Wicked Coeur d'Alene

Wicked Coeur d'Alene

Deborah Cuyle

Published by The History Press
Charleston, SC
www.historypress.com

First published 2021

Manufactured in the United States

ISBN 9781467149129

Library of Congress Control Number: 2021941605

Notice: The information in this book is true and complete to the best of our knowledge. It is offered without guarantee on the part of the author or The History Press. The author and The History Press disclaim all liability in connection with the use of this book.

I dedicate this book to everyone who loves Coeur d'Alene as much as I do! I also dedicate this book to everyone who believes Idaho is as beautiful as I think it is. I dedicate this book to all the Idaho history aficionados out there; I hope our paths cross someday if they haven't already.

As always, I dedicate this book to my mom, Roxie, who always believed I could do anything I set my mind to. She was seldom wrong.

CONTENTS

Preface 9
Acknowledgements 13
Introduction 15

1. Soiled Doves, Mining Men and Wild Women 23
2. Prohibition, Saloons and Intoxication 53
3. Pistols, Problems and Violence 79
4. Robbers, Gambling and Swindling 105
5. Labor Disputes, Revenge and Riots 123

Conclusion 151
Bibliography 153
About the Author 157

PREFACE

I hope readers will enjoy immersing themselves in the wicked history of old Coeur d'Alene. With all of my books, I try to incorporate as many historical facts, full names and dates as possible for each story. I feel this brings the characters to life and makes learning about the town more interesting. Many of my readers tell me they really enjoy learning about the town's history while reading about the local pioneers—their personal troubles, fears and accomplishments. With these true stories about early Coeur d'Alene, I hope to bring many of the local citizens, sneaky criminals and vigilantes, ladies of the night, barkeeps, hotel owners, bankers, politicians and everyone in between back to life. Otherwise, some of these people would have gone through their lives leaving no memories of themselves at all—except maybe a tombstone or an unmarked grave.

These true tales all actually occurred in the city of Coeur d'Alene or in the nearby towns. Other accounts are about people who only came through the Coeur d'Alenes in their travels, but they are such fascinating parts of the history of north Idaho that it would be a shame not to include them in this book.

It is interesting to learn how the police captured criminals and solved crimes in the old days; before the modern-day luxuries of forensics, DNA, fingerprints and databases. These brave and intelligent men often only had a tiny clue, such as a missing button, a footprint, gossip or hearsay (and hopefully confessions), to solve a crime. The lawmen in those days deserve a lot more credit and kudos than they probably ever received.

Commissioner Hayne, a Prohibition agent, trains his hooch hound—a dog trained to detect liquor. Here, the hound smells the flask of whiskey in his back pocket. *Courtesy of the Library of Congress, item no. 89707464.*

Note: *Thirty Years a Detective; A Thorough and Comprehensive Exposé of Criminal Practices of All Grades and Classes*, by Allan Pinkerton (1819–1884), is an interesting look at police investigative work and common crimes in the 1900s. (This book can be found on Internet Archive's website: www.archive.org.)

I currently live in the Coeur d'Alene region and have fallen in love with it, so this book hits home with me. I have great interest and an extreme respect for the early pioneers, combined with a personal fascination for local history and old buildings. I love reading about the first settlers of a town—everyone, from the Native tribes, to the soldiers, to the immigrants, to the shopkeepers...

It is fun to walk the same streets today that early settlers once walked and think about how it was back in the old days.

When I look at time-worn brick buildings or century-old hardwood floors, I try to imagine the thousands of people who once visited these buildings. I think of the strong horses that once pulled wagons and goods down the streets. I think of the gunslingers and outlaws, the bartenders and shopkeepers—all of them living their lives and going about their business, just as we all do today. I would have loved to have been alive back in the late 1800s.

Many of the stories in this book were pulled out of old newspapers, recapturing early Coeur d'Alene's fascinating history and unique characters. The book is not intended to be a nonfiction project, because even after hundreds of hours hunched over, reading and researching articles, I still found conflicting dates and inconsistent historic details, so please take it for what it is and just enjoy the read. This is ultimately a book about the many mischievous and wicked people and the interesting history of early Coeur d'Alene and the nearby towns nestled in the north Idaho Territory.

So, sit back with a glass of wine or cup of coffee and enjoy reading *Wicked Coeur d'Alene*!

ACKNOWLEDGEMENTS

There are many people to thank for this endeavor, and without their help and guidance, this book would not have been possible. My wonderful editor, Artie Crisp, has been such a pleasure to work with on my Coeur d'Alene books, along with all of the other incredible people at Arcadia Publishing and The History Press. Their mission to promote local history is passionate and infectious, and I am blessed to create my many books with them. Their dedication to recording local history is nothing less than amazing, and without them, many books would never be written.

My appreciation is extended to all those individuals who took the time to share local records and documents; without them, this book would not have the extra flair that I love so much.

And, as always, I want to thank every single person who does what they can to preserve history, whether it is volunteering at their local historical society, maintaining old cemeteries and gravestones that would otherwise be neglected or simply researching their private genealogy through sites like www.ancestry.com. In this fast-paced and high-tech world, the past can, unfortunately, be easily forgotten, and every effort to maintain and record valuable data, photographs, diaries, documents and records is of the utmost importance for future generations.

I also want to thank my followers and friends who have supported my craft all these years.

And of course, I want to thank my cat, Lily, for taking the time to walk across my keyboard right before I get a chance to save my work. She is always so helpful!

INTRODUCTION

Not many places in the United States can compete with the beauty of Coeur d'Alene, Idaho; its splendor is enhanced even more dramatically by the adjoining clear blue water and scenic mountains. The region's magnificence and charm attracted some of the wealthiest people in the United States. Many relocated and enjoyed the 135 miles of lake shores Coeur d'Alene offered. Soon, the town earned a fitting nickname from the elites who lived there: the "Scenic City by an Unsalted Sea."

Coeur d'Alene and the entire territory of northern Idaho are beyond beautiful, and people are moving there by the dozen. It is a city that prides itself on cleanliness, low crime, friendly people, great businesses and excellent restaurants. Curious travelers come to visit and end up looking for a house to buy.

But this book is not about that; it is a book about old Coeur d'Alene, before it became a bustling hub of Idaho excellence that nears perfection.

A lot of towns cropped up in Idaho around the late 1800s due to the mining of precious metals, lumber activity and the railroad expansion—or, like in the case of the Coeur d'Alene area, all three. And with these gainful elements came money-hungry pioneers in pursuit of fortune, but with that also came the underbellies of those who would profit from them in one way or another—prostitutes, robbers, gunmen, saloon owners, dance hall girls, pickpockets, opium den vendors, hotel proprietors and more. They all catered to anyone who had a few coins in their grip or a bill in their pocket. Some businesses literally followed the money from town to town. Their

This postcard of early Coeur d'Alene shows the beauty of the river and mountains, which was the draw for many citizens. *Courtesy of the Boston Public Library, from the Tichnor Brothers Collection.*

whole trade could be loaded or unloaded in a day, the actual structure being nothing more than a canvas tent. When the money ran dry, the venture would simply pack up its goods, load them on a horse-drawn wagon and off they'd go to the next profitable town.

However, some business owners decided to put down roots in Coeur d'Alene, unwilling to leave the town they then called their home. They did anything and everything within their grasp to remain profitable and permanent. Soon, a few more permanent buildings popped up in town: a general store, a brewery, the Coeur d'Alene Inn, the Fashion Saloon, Fatty Carrol's Dance Hall and Tony Tubb's Hotel d'Landing. At the time, Coeur d'Alene boasted that it had over twenty saloons to cater to locals and tourists.

One of the earliest known settlers in the area was a loudmouthed man named McAndrews, who always carried his gun. When McAndrews began drinking, swinging his gun around, yelling and carrying on, smart people hurried to the safety of their homes. One night, mouthy McAndrews's luck ran out, and a man shot him in the chest and ended his life right on the spot.

The first of several positions in town were quickly developed; the postmaster was V.W. Sander, the drugstore owner was Jack Couvaland, the blacksmith was James Tracy and one of the first carpenters was Sam Smith.

Makeshift towns like this one cropped up all over the United States due to gold and silver rushes. Sometimes, the businesses would disappear as quickly as they rose, as they followed miners and railroad men. *Courtesy of the National Archives at College Park, public domain,* Deadwood, South Dakota in 1876, *Wikimedia Commons.*

Visitors were constantly drawn to the picturesque lakeside area of Coeur d'Alene, a city that lured and beckoned people from everywhere. And once they arrived in Coeur d'Alene, they found they were unable to break away from its grasp—like an irresistible and delicious lover.

When one reads through old Coeur d'Alene newspapers, the same names flicker over the pages time and time again—people peddling their services and wares in the same way as folks do today. But I wonder who were these townspeople, really? No faded photographs of them can be found anywhere; perhaps their photographs were passed down to future generations, only to be eventually tossed into the garbage or accidentally lost. The only remaining evidence of their existence at all are the newspaper advertisements they placed in the *Coeur d'Alene Press* so long ago or possibly a short obituary written about them.

Who was M.J. Liddel besides the doctor and surgeon in town during 1892? Who was F.E. Armstrong besides the local barber? What did Ms. Kildea, one of the towns dressmakers, look like? As she threaded her needles and looked out into the streets of early Coeur d'Alene, did she miss her prior home or was she fleeing from an old way of life she would rather leave forgotten? No one really knows.

In 1896, Mr. J.H. Bethel sold jewelry and repaired watches (he also sold bicycles), and his little store was located on Sherman Avenue. Frank Bristow worked at the hardware store, and a faceless, hardworking man named R.R. Mann took care of horses' hooves as the town's blacksmith, his noisy shop located on Fourth Street, next to Y.W. Sanders & Company (located on the southeast corner of Fourth and Sherman Streets).

Do you need a doctor? Go see C.H. Henkle. Do you need a dentist? S.H. McEuen is your man. Do you have legal troubles? James Graham is at your service.

These Coeur d'Alene pioneers probably never dreamed that over one hundred years later, their names would end up in a book.

One of the most important services provided to any town was that of the local druggist. Arthur L. Miller was one of the go-to guys in Coeur d'Alene if one suffered from ailments. He ran the local pharmacy, where one could discreetly purchase pills for everything from dropsy to consumption, from piles to constipation. If you didn't like him, you could hit up druggist Mr. J. Schermanson for his pharmaceutical selections and compounds.

A best seller in the day was a tablet called "A Women's Friend," which touted it could cure headaches, backaches and weakness, and (if one took enough of them) it was said to "give you health and strength and make your life a pleasure!" Now, who wouldn't want that?

Opium, snake oil, cocaine and vibrators were all common remedies in this era, and no prescriptions were even needed for the purchase of opium or cocaine. Snake oil was said to be the miracle elixir of life (though, later, it was proven to be fraudulent). Cocaine was the fifteen-cent instant cure for toothaches, depression, sinus troubles, alcoholism and impotence (it

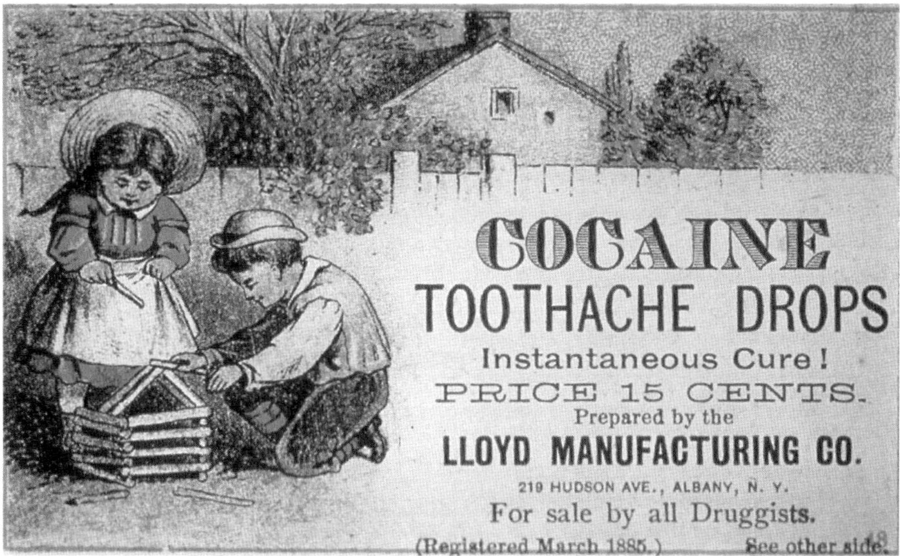

In the old days, cocaine was the fifteen-cent instant cure for toothaches, depression, sinus troubles, alcoholism and even impotence. *Courtesy of the National Library of Medicine.*

was more likely the patient just didn't really care anymore about their ailments after a dose of cocaine). The popular cure for hysteria among women was the introduction of the electric massage vibrator, guaranteed to also cure dozens of other ailments in men and women.

By the late 1800s, upper-class White women made up more than 60 percent of opium addicts. "Uterine and ovarian complications cause more ladies to fall into the [opium] habit than all other diseases combined," wrote Dr. Frederick Heman Hubbard in his 1881 book, *The Opium Habit and Alcoholism.* Chinese opium dens were popular in most cities, as they ran hand in hand with the saloons and brothels in Coeur d'Alene.

Over one hundred years later, it seems as though not much has really changed. People still struggle. People still want to be happy and get relief from their troubles and pain. Yet, it seems that no matter how bad things get, people will still want to eat, drink and have sex.

Murder, public drunkenness, shoot-outs, robberies, jealous rages, accidents, legal battles, escapes from prison, prostitution, gambling—the pioneers faced the same destructive vices that we suffer from today.

But the brand-new, beautiful and irresistible town of Coeur d'Alene desired to keep these problems under wraps in the hopes of luring mining and lumber money (and the influence it afforded) to the area. Like many up-

The new cure for hysteria among women was the electric massage vibrator—guaranteed to also cure dozens of other ailments in both men and women. *Courtesy of Smith Lindstro, and the National Library of Medicine.*

and-coming cities, Coeur d'Alene wanted to portray the image of offering a perfect lifestyle in its enticing and alluring waterside town so that big-money people would come from all over the world—and they did. Coeur d'Alene was so spectacular (and still is today) that, in truth, not much could have kept anyone who had the means to move there from doing so.

Yet, as much as Coeur d'Alene wanted to render a pristine Charles Dickens–like atmosphere to the thriving city, reality still existed. For its first several years of settlement, the area near Fort Sherman and the Coeur d'Alene River was riddled with troubles and was considered a rough-and-tumble town—it was rumored to be one of the roughest around.

The newspapers echo tales of desperate gamblers, prostitutes and prospectors who did everything they could to secure their own future at all costs. If the walls could talk in the buildings that still stand in Coeur d'Alene, they would whisper dark tales of hushed murders, illegal gambling and secretive drinking (during Prohibition), corrupt politics and labor disputes.

Interesting Idaho characters emerge, like May Hutton, a women's suffrage supporter whose rival, Emma DeVoe, tried to ruin her reputation by publicizing May's previous life as "Bootleg Mary" and that she had run a "bad house for immoral purposes." Fatty Carroll is another notorious bad guy in Coeur d'Alene's history. He was the well-known (and scary) proprietor of Carroll's Variety, as well as the owner of several saloons, opium dens, cathouses and gambling halls. Fatty was quick to kill anyone he didn't like—their bodies to be buried in shallow graves nearby. Some bones of his victims are possibly still being found today.

A unique and favorite local was Mr. Salis Smith, another one of the city's druggists. On a mission to keep everyone happy, he created combinations to cure almost everything, from headaches to menstrual cramps. Not surprisingly, his wares were often 50 percent alcohol, mixed with a just little bit of cocaine or opium to boot.

In *Wicked Coeur d'Alene*, these and many other stories will be shared. Tales of old-fashioned wickedness and the mischievous people who once lived and thrived in Coeur d'Alene, as well as northern part of Idaho, will finally be exposed.

Interesting Fact: Ever wonder how Idaho got its name? In 1860, a man who worked with the miners suggested the name *Idaho* because it meant "gem of the mountains." The territory was rich with many precious stones and valuable minerals. Everyone seemed to like the name, except the United States Senate, which rejected it because it was not an "Indian" word. (They decided to call it Colorado instead.) Yet, the name Idaho continued to be popular with the locals, and on March 4, 1863, Congress reluctantly accepted the name Idaho for the territory.

1

SOILED DOVES, MINING MEN AND WILD WOMEN

Sex—since the beginning of time, it has been one of the most powerful influences known to man and woman. The hard life lived by most working woman in the old days was nothing to brag about. Unless they married into money and luxury or were born into a family of wealth, they had to struggle daily to have a place to sleep and have things to drink and eat. They did not really have welfare or charity back then, so if they didn't work, they didn't eat—end of story. Some could rely on the generosity of churches or neighbors, but since soiled doves were frowned upon by women in the community and most likely did not go to church, it left a lot of women abandoned to survive by their own means. Unfortunately, this meant selling their bodies for ten-cent pieces. They also typically resorted to crime to supplement their income, whether that meant getting clients drunk and then robbing them blind after sex or simply encouraging men to drink more because they were getting a percentage of the profits.

Some women who refused to ply the sex trade took to doing laundry and cooking for the soldiers or tourists. Others became employees of the soldier camps, local saloons or busy hotels.

In the young mining towns, often, the extreme ratio of men to women was two hundred to one. These were not good odds for a horny man, but it was a great place of business for the brothel owner. Most towns had a more reasonable ratio of fifty to one.

At one time, there were over four hundred prostitutes in Coeur d'Alene, and brothels were very profitable businesses for the saloons and madams. *Courtesy of the Library of Congress, item no. 93505160.*

With the discovery of silver or gold came money, and when payday came, the men were eager to spend it on booze, gambling and women. Prostitution, for some lucky women, meant a world in which they could control their destiny and finances. They could literally go from rags to riches in a couple of years if they played their cards right and were careful with their money.

It was common for working women to get a man to buy drinks for both themselves and the women (at inflated prices). The women would get a cut of the profits (termed "box rustling"), and if not, the chances of rolling (robbing) the man after he was satisfied for the night was always a possibility. If a working girl was lucky, she could get under the rule of a kind madam and at least enjoy some safety and security.

Prostitution was looked on by the public as a "necessary evil," and most turned a blind eye to it. The more respectable ladies of the night often were very generous in the community and supplied items for local schools and city services. The lower-class soiled doves who worked in dirty, cramped and cheap tents or cribs were in survival mode, and many ended up addicted to drugs, became suicidal or were even murdered. The life of a prostitute, for most of the women, meant to live in constant fear, as the chances of an unwanted pregnancy, disease or assault were ever present. Birth control for women during this era was not yet a science or the process of simply taking a little white pill every day as prescribed by a proper doctor. Unfortunately, for the women of that era, they often had risky means of "birth control," administered by the ladies themselves (or their madams). Douching with a solution of carbolic acid, ergot and oil of tansy was often the only protection available. In the worst case of an unwanted pregnancy, the horrible aspect of infanticide sometimes came into play.

One of the earliest known dance halls in the Coeur d'Alene area in 1884 was in a little town of less than thirty buildings known as Littlefield (formerly called Butte City, near the town of Murray and the area termed Butte Gulch, east of Coeur d'Alene). Although the town had little accommodations in the way of a real road and was nestled in the middle of the woods west of nowhere, its dance hall still managed to draw the men. Since the ladies living there were outnumbered, it was necessary for them to rotate and change partners frequently in order to please the male crowd. For a small fee, each man was afforded one trip around the dance floor with the lady of their choice.

In the 1890s, madams in Idaho applied for and received liquor licenses for their establishments. This allowed them to legally sell overpriced liquor to their patrons. When things got tough, some female business owners were forced to sell or lease their belongings to stay afloat. Madams could also "mortgage" their possessions, pianos or any other valuable items if they were

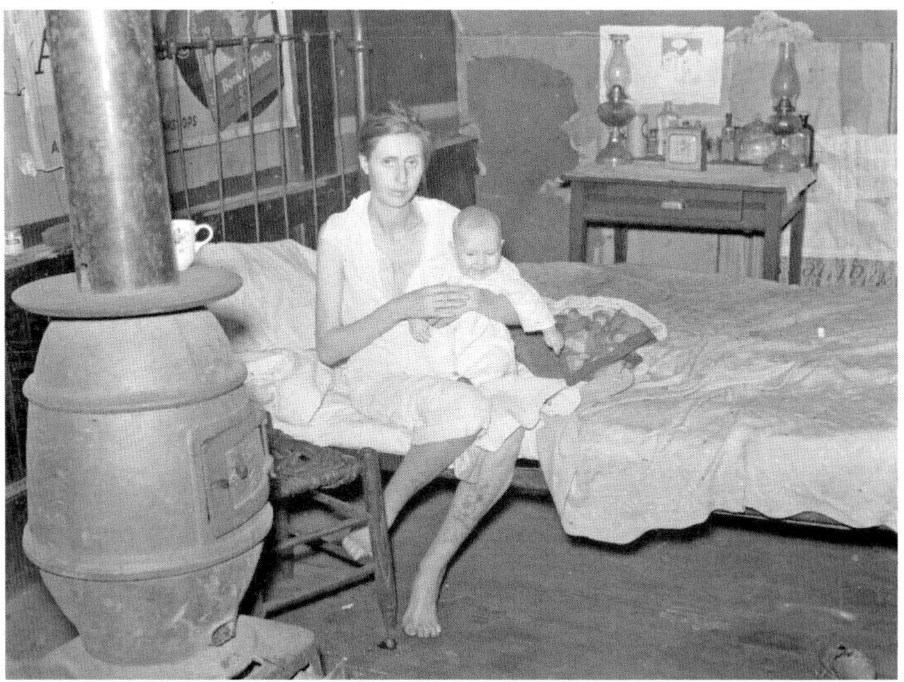

Above: This unidentified prostitute is living a tragic lifestyle. Prostitutes often had babies out of wedlock, contracted syphilis or other diseases and frequently committed suicide. *Courtesy of the Library of Congress, item no. 2017799370; photographer, Marion Post Wolcott.*

Opposite: The seductive lure of the beautiful dance hall ladies left men speechless and their pockets empty! *Courtesy of Wikimedia Commons; artist, Roland, 1890.*

in need of money. Interestingly, a notorious madam named Gracie Adams of the Star Brothel in the nearby town of Wallace, at one time, mortgaged a "gilded-frame mirror, crystal wine glasses and decanters, satin pillow shams and eighteen satin comforters." It does not report how much money she was actually given for these valuable items.

As Coeur d'Alene grew, men ultimately began controlling the liquor stores, brothels, dance halls and theaters. Even though the men began owning these establishments, it was still mostly the women who ran them. In the early 1900s, nineteen saloons were directly linked to prostitution in Coeur d'Alene, and the same twelve men owned most of these establishments.

Most citizens looked the other way when it came to "female boardinghouses" (brothels) in their towns, but after some huffing by certain individuals, tall fences were built around the cribs and female boarding facilities to keep the dreadful situation out of the public eye.

Beautiful women were sometimes scarce in the old mining towns, and the pretty ones were either high-end prostitutes or high-society women. *Courtesy of www.pictures.net, free to use through public domain.*

Between 1880 and 1911, over four hundred prostitutes worked in the Coeur d'Alene region of Idaho.

By 1909, the Tenth Idaho State Legislature passed a law making it a misdemeanor for a proprietor to allow a woman to enter any business that sold intoxicating beverages; that did not go over very well with the women.

After many arguments, the Supreme Court later decided that women could enter saloons, provided they entered for lawful purposes and not just to get drunk, sell themselves or cause trouble.

As for the prostitutes of that generation, hundreds of these poor women ended up in unmarked graves, the only tangible memory of them being a slight blurb in the local newspaper about a nameless local girl who committed suicide and suffered death due to consuming carbolic acid mixed with morphine, the morphine relieving the pain she felt while swallowing the carbolic acid.

SOILED DOVES

Bronco Liz and Her Cheating Husband

The Coeur d'Alene region had a famous working girl whose real name was Ione Jane Whitney Skeels, but she was nicknamed "Bronco Liz" (date of birth and death unknown). As she did not ride horses, one can only speculate as to how she acquired her nickname. She supposedly competed with two other famous north Idaho ladies of the night, Molly b'Damn and Terrible Edith. Liz was known as the local dance hall queen and a popular male entertainer.

Liz met her soon-to-be husband, Charles "Chas" W. Skeels (1860–1889), while he was working with the Coeur d'Alene mines and entertaining the miners. Skeels had originally come from Huntingtonshire, England, and crossed the sea in 1871 to make his new life in New York City before heading west. At the time of their attraction, Mr. Skeels had a wife and two children at home, and their affair had to be kept secret. Skeels was so in love with Liz that he enticed her to marry him as soon as he was granted a divorce from his then-current wife. He devised a wild plan to do this: he suggested she cut off all of her hair, dress in men's clothing and go to work on his family's ranch in Choteau, Montana, until he could finalize his divorce.

Liz agreed to the arrangement, and soon, she became a working hand instead of a working girl. She continued to work on the farm, with no one the wiser that she was actually a girl. After several months, Skeels did get his divorce, and the couple went to Moscow, Idaho, to get hitched on January 2, 1888.

Instead of the honeymoon Liz expected, Skeels sent her back to Montana to "wait" for him. She did so suspiciously until February came around. The new bride had a feeling something was up.

The couple then moved to Coeur d'Alene and were living in a rented room in the Union Block in town. Skeels told her he was extremely busy conducting business, as he had become the proprietor of the Pantheon Saloon. Liz soon caught wind of a rumor that Skeels was sleeping with another woman, an actress named Frankie Howard who worked at the Theater Comique. They met often at her love nest in a building known as Actor's Flat at 412 Howard Street in Spokane.

Liz became furious and went to find her husband but not before getting her hands on a pistol (she had shot him once before while they were in Cascade, Montana). Liz's choice of weapon was a .32-caliber British Bulldog revolver that she had found at a pawn shop. The broker emptied the cartridge, but Liz was so determined to teach her husband a lesson that she roamed the district until she finally found someone to load the gun for her.

Liz worked out a plan to trick her cheating husband into coming out of hiding. She called for a messenger boy. She paid him to look for Skeels and give an urgent message to him that he was needed at home because she was not feeling well. The boy quickly ran around town, looking for the bamboozling husband, but Skeels was not in any of the saloons in town.

Furious, Liz took matters into her own hands.

Liz and the boy traveled over to the Flats to scare her husband.

After much knocking on the apartment's entry by the boy, a very frustrated Skeels finally opened up the door. Disgruntled and irritated at

Bronco Liz used a pocket revolver like this .32-caliber British Bulldog to shoot her cheating husband, Charles Skeels. *Courtesy of Wikimedia Commons, photograph by Rama.*

being interrupted, Skeels left the room and entered the hallway, where Liz was waiting for him. Knowing he was caught red-handed, Skeels instantly became afraid of Liz, as she had shot him once before during their relationship.

He put up his hands and said, "Don't you make any breaks at me—keep away! I'm through with you forever!"

Liz did not listen. She fired the pistol at him, and three bullets entered his body. One went through his left arm and lodged in his stomach. The second bullet hit his right side. The third one secured a spot in his lower back.

Skeels yelled, "Let up firing your gun, Liz, or you will kill me!"

Liz looked her husband straight in the eyes, and without any hesitation, she pulled the trigger.

The fourth bullet somehow went wayward—luckily for Skeels.

Without further ado, Liz promptly turned on her heels and calmly made her way out from the Flats and headed back home. Skeels, somehow unaware of the extent of damage she had done to him, slowly followed her. But he didn't get far. Bleeding profusely, he had to stop at Nelson's doorstep. A man named D.S. Cowgill heard Skeels moaning as he cried out, "Some of you gentlemen, help me!"

As the blood slowly drained from his body, a carriage was called. After ten or fifteen minutes, the carriage arrived and took him to his saloon. The men carried him upstairs, where he wanted to lie down. A very rough-looking woman answered the door, possibly a working girl from the Pantheon. Soon, Drs. Essig and Parmlee attended to his wounds, but they both thought the shots were fatal and that he would surely soon be dead.

Officer Gillespie made his way to Liz and promptly told her she was under arrest and kept her confined to her residence until Sheriff Glispin and Officer McKernam could take her off to jail.

The *Spokane Falls Review* noted that she told them, "Of course I won't deny I shot him, but I was driven to it. I was crazy with jealousy! Since I married him, he has never been true. I met him in the Coeur d'Alene mines…when I heard he was now living with a woman named Alice somebody, and it made me wild!"

T.W. Murphy and Thomas Griffits were hired to defend poor Mrs. Skeels, also known as Bronco Liz.

The philandering Mr. Skeels died from his wounds the next day while resting at his son Alfred's home. He was surrounded by his mom, three brothers and his two children from a former wife.

The trial for his murder lasted nine days, and the jury deliberated for forty-eight hours. The jury found Liz not guilty, and she was acquitted. They felt the verdict was justified by the evidence that Skeels was a bad man and a danger to the community.

Even if Skeels was considered locally a bad man, almost five hundred people attended his funeral.

The *Lewiston Teller* reported on January 2, 1890, that one reporter said, "We don't believe Liz should have been hanged, but she should have been punished to some extent."

It is said that Hell has no fury like a woman scorned—and that appears to be true.

A Red-Light District Raid that Became a Wedding

During the summer of 1908, Patrolmen Evans and Steele had had enough of the shabby house of ill repute run by H.J. Baker and Mrs. D. Baker (her real name was Dollie E. Grant) and their partner, Orvey Mitchell (who ran the Spokane Bar in Coeur d'Alene). After several unheeded warnings, the cops decided it was time for a raid.

The notorious house of prostitution on Tubbs Hill in Coeur d'Alene caused nearby locals to become agitated. The last complaint was filed by the manager of the Coeur d'Alene Lumber Mill. He was sick and tired of the drunken men loitering through his lot at all hours of the night, looking for sex. What bothered him most was their constant tossing of burning cigar stubs and cigarettes onto the ground of the mill. It was a valid complaint, as a fire in a lumber mill (or anywhere, for that matter) was surely to be devastating and could destroy the whole town.

The three were taken to jail and booked. Mrs. Baker was charged with prostitution. A flustered Baker appeared before the judge and promptly showed him their marriage license. Mrs. Baker could not be a prostitute, as she was Mr. Baker's wife. He and Dollie were married in Montana for ten years before moving to Coeur d'Alene—the certificate proved it. Upon inspecting the license, the judge told Baker that they were not married under that particular license. The surprised couple looked at the judge in disbelief.

The judge must have been in a grand mood that day, because he actually let the criminals leave his courtroom so they could drive to the county seat to secure a new marriage license. To everyone's amazement, when the couple returned promptly, the judge even offered to marry them. The impromptu wedding ceremony was commenced at 10:00 a.m. that same day.

But it was not all was fun and celebration. After everything was over and the couple was married for real this time, the judge still charged them with running a house of prostitution.

Not surprisingly, their partner, Orvey Mitchell, failed to appear in court for his trial. Later, Mitchell was arrested, along with his wife, Maude, and Judge Main ordered them to close their other house of ill repute.

The Glencoe: Coeur d'Alene's House of Ill Repute

It was recorded that, at one time, there were over four hundred prostitutes in the Coeur d'Alene region. Wherever there was money being made, there were bound to be prostitutes cashing in on that fortune. And there was plenty of money being made in the area.

One of the local brothels was called the Glencoe. In October 1908, the red-light district was under scrutiny from locals and officers. During this particular raid, Mr. and Mrs. Shomers were the targets. They admitted they ran the Glencoe House in Coeur d'Alene and were soon to be charged with several other crimes. Once arrested, Helen Shomers was held in jail for thirty-six hours. Judge Chamberlain wanted to make sure that she was charged with adultery. Her husband, Mike Shomers, was detained on vagrancy charges, with the bail set at $300, a price the judge knew Shomers could never pay. After all was said and done, the judge threatened Mr. Shomers with a choice of thirty days in the slammer or leaving Coeur d'Alene immediately.

Shomers chose to leave town. Helen was released from jail due to the weird mistake that in the thirty-six hours she was being held, no one ever officially notified her of what actual charge had been brought against her. At the frustration of Judge Chamberlain, she was ultimately set free.

In reality, it was discovered that the Shomers were arrested and detained because the police believed that Mr. Shomer was involved in the tragic Franklin Hotel fire that destroyed the entire building, all of its contents and threatened the city a few weeks before. The fire also killed two men, Gus Layton and Jacob Skogland, who were staying at the hotel that tragic night. Mike Shomers stated that he had been staying at the Franklin Hotel that night, but during the fire, he was at the Lakeview Bar, drinking. He only ran back to the hotel after he got word that it was on fire to retrieve his belongings. By the time he arrived, the entire hotel was up in flames.

Apparently, at that time, they could not acquire any hard evidence against Mr. Shomer to keep him in jail on the arson charge.

North Idaho Legendary Prostitute: Molly b'Damn

Not all prostitutes had a bad life. The most famous north Idaho madam was named Molly b'Damn (1853–1888); she earned a great living and was highly respected in her small community. Molly b'Damn was one of the most well-known female figures of the Coeur d'Alene region (and still is today). Molly b'Damn was a pioneer woman who came to Murray in 1884 and quickly became a business owner, taking up Cabin no. 1 without question. Cabin no. 1 was well known as the madam's residence, and it was apparently vacant during the time of her arrival.

Although she ran a house of ill repute, she was very considerate of her new community and immediately became well loved by everyone. Although she was basically uneducated, she could quote Shakespeare, Dante and Milton. Molly (whose real name was Maggie Hall) was a high-spirited prostitute turned local heroine during a local smallpox epidemic. Ultimately, the selfless act of caring for others would be her demise.

Born on December 26, 1853, in Dublin, Ireland, the legendary Molly b'Damn came to the United States at the age of twenty in 1873. Fleeing from the residual results of the famine that plagued Ireland in 1845 (the failed potato crops led to the deaths of about 750,000 people), Molly was one of many who headed to New York to start a new life. A year later, she married a man named Burdan, and for some reason, she changed her first name to Molly. Tiring of her husband's antics, Molly left him and traveled the states in search of her next adventure. In 1884, Molly became greatly interested in the recent gold discovery in the Coeur d'Alene Mountains.

During the long ride through the mountains, Molly discovered a woman and her child sitting in the snow, almost freezing to death. Not a single person on the trail cared if these people lived or died—except for Molly. She piled all of them onto her horse and proceeded until they came to a small shelter, where they stopped for the night. All of them freezing cold, Molly wrapped the strangers in her extra coats, and they tried to sleep until the next morning.

At sunrise, Molly, the woman and child rode, shivering, into the small town of Murray, Idaho. In Murray, Molly introduced herself to a local man named Phil O'Rourke, who took a liking to her, but with her thick Irish accent, her name sound like Molly b'Damn instead of Molly Burdan, thus her new nickname was created. Molly felt right at home in Murray and decided to stay.

Molly was more than just a madam. She was a true businesswoman. One of Molly's favorite moneymakers was a large tub filled with hot water that she would place in the middle of the street (this would always coincide with the miner's payday). Knowing that the men had money in their pockets, Molly would tease the men. She would parade around the street, scantily dressed, and would tell the men to sprinkle some gold dust into the bath tub, and when the bottom of the tub had a nice, sparkly thin layer of gold, she would strip down naked and immerse her lovely body into the water.

Well, the men could not resist her charm, and one after the other, they would sprinkle a little of their gold dust into the bathtub. And, being the businesswoman she was, for an additional fee, the men could scrub her lovely backside.

Murray, known as the "Cradle City of the Coeur d'Alenes" in the late 1800s, was a base camp for prospectors who were hoping to strike it rich. The gold rush in the area prompted men to flock to the nearby Eagle Camp, which sprang up overnight (and was just as quickly abandoned in favor of nearby Murray) in the hopes of striking it rich. Even the legendary Wyatt Earp (1848–1929); his wife, Josie; and his brother James came to the area with the news of the discovery of gold. The cluster of small towns called Eagle City, Murray and Prichard soon reached a population of more than ten thousand people. The Earp brothers erected a large circus tent and ran it as the White Elephant Saloon. It is even rumored that Calamity Jane herself was in charge of organizing the first social and dance event in Eagle City.

Wyatt unfortunately challenged several local mine claims, including those of local A.J. Prichard. Wyatt wanted the claims named Consolidated Grizzly Bear, the Dividend, the Dead Scratch and the Golden Gate. Wyatt purchased a cabin on Eagle Street, lot 57, from a man named William Buzard in May 1884. Wyatt left town in a hurry and still owed about ten dollars in back taxes. Since Earp lost his court battle against Prichard, it is a local legend that Wyatt was scheduled to be hanged in Murray for claim jumping. It's no wonder the Earps left town so quickly.

Molly opened her own tavern called the Acion Saloon, where Wyatt Earp's wife, Josie, often entertained guests. In December 1885, she sold the Acion Saloon lot to a woman named Mrs. C.R. Boyce.

When the dreaded smallpox hit Idaho in 1886, Molly wasted no time tending to the sick. Unfortunately, her kindness did not shelter her from getting sick herself. In 1888, Molly was weakened by consumption and died. Her final words were: "My real name is Maggie Hall. It was the name of my mother. She was a wonderful and good woman." She died on January 17, 1888, and over one thousand people followed her casket through town, each mourning the death of a much-loved local woman. She was known locally as the "Patron Saint of Murray."

Unfortunately, there are no known photographs of Molly b'Damn. The famous image of her that is plastered all over the internet has recently been said to be false. (It is rumored that one true photograph of Molly exists that was found inside of a wall in a building that was being remodeled in Murray some years ago. Unfortunately, the picture has long since disappeared, never to be made public.) The town of Murray has named its favorite annual festival the Molly b'Damn Gold Rush Days in her honor, and people come from all over to enjoy the three-day jubilee. Molly b'Damn was buried in the local cemetery, just a mile or so from town.

Molly b'Damn was one of the most famous prostitutes in the Coeur d'Alene region, and even today, there are festivals devoted to her. *Courtesy of the author.*

The following is an excerpt from Molly's eulogy that was clipped to her death records in the Murray Courthouse:

Maggie Hall has gone from our midst, but she will never be forgotten, living forever in our hearts a woman so strong, so forthright that only her good deeds will be remembered. Generous to a fault with her worlds goods, and with her bodily strength, she was one in whom no sacrifice was too great. She was a ministering angel to the sick and suffering.

MINING MEN

Thousands of men flocked to the Coeur d'Alene region in search of wealth untold. In 1883, in the Thompson Falls area alone, over five thousand men camped and began prospecting. The town was nothing but a few clumsy tents before the gold rush came. Soon, over twenty saloons littered the town, all eager to serve booze to the men. The women had other plans in mind. They would get the men drunk, and then, on the pretense of sex, they would

A group of hardworking unidentified miners take a minute to pose in 1910. The conditions underground were very dangerous, and many miners developed lead poisoning. *Courtesy of the Library of Congress, item no. 2014690192, Bain News Service.*

take them into the back and secretly rob them. A famous local card sharp named Jack McDonald had his share of fun in the region when he visited. During the mining boom, the ratio of men to women was once 50 to 1—no wonder the brothels were such a profitable business.

Stumpy Wicks Forever in Search of Gold

One odd fellow who spent his entire life in the Coeur d'Alene Mountains searching for gold was a man named Stumpy Wicks. He roamed the mountains, searching for fortune, his entire life. Not much was known about Stumpy. He had no family, no wife and no home—a sad and lonely existence. His death was swift, as he caught mountain fever. He died just three days after contracting the disease. Also called Rocky Mountain spotted fever or black measles, the disease was first described in the late 1880s and was very common in the Bitterroot Valley of Idaho. It is a bacterial infection caused by the bite of an infected tick. If left untreated, it attacks the kidneys and heart and becomes fatal. Stumpy died from this because it was left untreated.

Stumpy traveled the mountains alone for over forty years, and many people knew him. When he died, his fellow gold hunters made him a wooden coffin, placed an old flour sack over his face and buried him with a few kind words. They pulled some money together to hire a local priest for his last rites. His headstone was simply his name scratched on a rock.

Over forty men showed up for the makeshift funeral. In the pocket of his worn-out clothes, they found a photograph of an unknown woman. Who was this lady—a sister, mother, friend, lover? No one ever knew who the woman was in the photograph Stumpy held so dear.

Although not much was known about Stumpy—his beginnings or his life—the announcement of his death reached newspapers all over the states. His obituary was printed everywhere—Idaho, Texas, New Mexico, Nevada, Indiana, Nebraska, Montana, Illinois, Georgia, South Dakota, Virginia and Washington, D.C. For a man who held no history or personal connections, his funeral notice sure was printed widely.

Who Stumpy Wicks really was is a mystery. Curiously, in 1906, a woman named Alice McGowan wrote a story printed in the *Black Cat*, a collection of short stories, called "Stumpy Wicks and the Maverick."

Mining Men and Mine Owners

One man who was primarily responsible for causing trouble among the mining men was called Bodie Bill (his real name was William Doyle). Bill came to Coeur d'Alene from Arizona around 1892. A few years before, Bill and his brother had been run out of Nevada for running a gang that killed an innocent miner who refused to sell his claim to them. Bill decided right then and there to "kill all members of organized labor unions!" That would be quite the task, as there were thousands of union members.

But Bill got as far as he could with his plan. After the mining riots and troubles of 1892, the mine owners in Idaho took a chance on Bodie Bill and hired him on to intimidate and intentionally distill fear into the minds of the mining men. They wanted to ward off any attempts of the miners to demand higher wages. A group called the Mushroom Mining Men's Association (3Ms) had been formed recently to disrupt organized labor. Their plan was to control the entire county by creating a monopoly; they would make millions and get rid of any man who did not want to comply with their rules, caused trouble or outlived their usefulness. It was determined that the 3Ms would place spies among the men and purposely irritate them. They created a man to hate (one they had selected together that they felt they needed to be rid of), who would confront and bully the man until he ran off—then they would shoot him. The shooter was actually a member of the 3Ms group, but the miners were led to believe he was one of them, a miner. Bodie would sometimes claim that the murder was an accident and that his gun mysteriously went off.

Bodie Bill was a horrible person. He enjoyed power and manipulation. He was always brainstorming the next way to control the miners. He eagerly accepted the job as the manager for the 3Ms for a salary of $600 a month. He also wanted a percentage of the property that was controlled by the 3Ms.

To demonstrate his power and fearlessness, one day, Bodie Bill went into a local saloon on payday. He knew the bar would be full of miners drinking away their paychecks. He put his two guns on top of the bar and challenged any man to a duel. He said, "There are two guns here, one for myself and the other for any one of you sons of bitches who will take it and use it!" None of the men accepted his dangerous challenge. They knew Bodie Bill was an excellent shot and had killed men before for less.

It was rumored that Bill often wore a "shirt of mail," a homemade bullet-proof type of armor made by looping together over twenty-four thousand metal links, creating a heavy and cumbersome vest. There

Several unidentified miners worked together deep underground in cramped and very hazardous conditions—ones that often proved fatal. *Courtesy of the Library of Congress, item no. 2012648315; photographer, S.A. Noyes.*

would only be one reason to wear a shirt of mail every day—you were expecting to get shot.

The murder of a miner named Kneebone in July 1894 was said to be part of the 3Ms' plan. They felt he was a traitor and a spy, but the stories about Kneebone conflict.

Another man who met his maker was named Fred Whitney. Whitney was a well-liked and highly respected foreman of a mill. (He was also the nephew of a big-time stockholder.) Just a couple of months into his new job, six masked men showed up at his house at 10:00 p.m. and shot him in the leg. The injury was so bad that the doctors had to amputate his leg, which became infected, and poor Whitney died the next day. A $17,000 reward was offered for the capture and arrest of Whitney's killers. Detectives came from far and wide, hoping to solve the crime and collect the handsome reward, but no one was ever arrested. There were rumors of false leads and misinformation given out by the 3Ms themselves to keep the detectives on the wrong track and out of their hair as they moved on to other crimes.

Bodie was said to angrily repeat that he was going to "wipe the Coeur d'Alene miners off the face of the Earth!"

Tough man Bodie surprisingly loved to drink champagne. His favorite was Mumms Extra Dry. He frequently ordered it by the case from the nearby McLoughlin's Drugstore. The slippery man was also known to keep dead men on the payroll and skim money, fuel and supplies from the company.

He had plans to play the miners against one another with the wages they received, causing disputes and anger between the men. He devised a plan to blow up a mine so that the governor would declare martial law; then they would have military presence in the Coeur d'Alene Mountains to protect them. He demanded the 3Ms to spend a whopping $265,000 to fight the Coeur d'Alene Miners Association. His plotting seemed to never end.

The association decided to pay the miners two different sets of wages (a ridiculous $1.50 less per day, and miners were already working for only $3.50 per ten-hour day, and the shovelers were paid just $3.00), even though they worked just a few miles from one another. Men would get into fights, and when the frightened and angry men would run or walk away from him, Bodie yelled he would "shoot them on the spot!" And sometimes, he would.

The Bunker Hill and Sullivan Mine after the horrific explosion in 1899 that was caused by the mining riots. The miners did not want to work for less than the agreed $3.50 per day. *Courtesy of Idaho State Archives, item no. P1964-157-10, public domain.*

An aerial view of the rebuilt Bunker Hill and Sullivan Mine. *Courtesy of the National Archives and Records Administration, public domain, Wikimedia Commons.*

It was told that a miner's death could be passed off as being caused by the man's own carelessness, making the company in no way responsible for his untimely death. Even local coroners were bought off by the association to say that the death was an accident—corruption and greed at its finest.

All of the craziness of the recent ongoing mining wars came to a head on April 29, 1899, when hundreds of rioters went to the Bunker Hill and Sullivan Mine with over three thousand pounds of dynamite, determined to blow it up—which they did.

After the April 29 fiasco, Idaho State and the United States Army decided to punish the rioters and determined that "no union men could work in the Coeur d'Alene region" until further notice. The men were arrested on "any old charge," rounded up and put in a makeshift bullpen, since there were too many men to put in the local jail. Extreme trouble brewed between the miners and mine owners—and it was only going to get worse.

The Horrors of the Bullpen

One of the worst ideas during the second run of troublesome times was the implementation of the new bullpen (a temporary jail). There was a similar bullpen used during the 1892 riots, but this bullpen was considered even worse.

The large number of union men who were arrested after the Bunker Hill and Sullivan Mine explosion were thrown into what was literally just a large cow barn. Governor Frank Steunenberg announced that he "promised to punish and totally eradicate from this community a class of criminals who, for years, have been committing murders and other crimes in open violation of the law." Those words would ultimately be the death of him years later.

The new bullpen consisted of an old barn, sheds and railroad cars that could hold around 350 men. The cows' wooden feeding troughs became the men's uncomfortable beds. To make matters worse, the men were not even given blankets. They had no coats. At one time, the men went for thirty-six hours without food or water. They had to eat off the dirty, muddy floor. The

The bullpen could hold 350 men, although 600 men were eventually imprisoned there. Cow troughs became beds, and the men had no blankets or coats. *Photograph from* The Coeur d'Alenes; or, a Tale of the Modern Inquisition in Idaho, *by May Arkwright Hutton, 1900, self-published. No copyright extension, photographer unknown.*

In the bullpen, the men went thirty-six hours without food or water and ate off the floor. The union members suffered from lice and malnutrition. *Photograph from* The Coeur d'Alenes; or, a Tale of the Modern Inquisition in Idaho, *by May Arkwright Hutton, 1900, self-published. No copyright extension, photographer unknown.*

hardworking union members were literally treated worse than hogs. In order to keep the men in the dark on current events, they could not receive mail or read the newspapers.

The arrests continued, additional men were detained, and soon, the bullpen was housing 660 men. The pen was enclosed with barbed wire, and there were no toilets, just some chicken coops. The men could not bathe, so soon, they were plagued with lice. They received two meals per day: at 9:00 a.m., they got bread, bacon and coffee; and at 2:30 p.m., they were fed stew, beans and bread.

Although most of the men were released within a few weeks, on May 12, there were still 450 men confined to the bullpen. On May 30, that number went down to 194. By October 10, there were only 65 men left imprisoned. The last men were finally released from the bullpen in December, after suffering from malnourishment, abuse, insects and disease. Of the 1,200 men arrested for the riot and destruction, only one man, Paul Corcoran, went to trial. Corcoran was found guilty and sentenced to seventeen years in the state penitentiary.

Because of the destruction of the mine, martial law continued to remain in force, and no miner was allowed to work in the district without a state permit. In order to get a permit, the miner had to prove they took no part in the demolition of the mine. No members of the Western Federation of Miners Union could get a permit until they quit their former membership.

After all was said and done, the bullpen was moved and repurposed for housing cavalry horses, the crude treatment of the miners sadly and quickly forgotten.

Note: *The Coeur d'Alenes: Or a Tale of the Modern Inquisition in Idaho*, written and published by May Arkwright Hutton herself, tells more about the bullpen and the mining troubles during that period. After the book was published, May ran around and collected and destroyed as many copies of the book as she could find—probably because she exposed a lot of dirty politics and shady characters within its three hundred pages and later thought better of it. (This book can be found on Internet Archive's website: www.archive.org.)

Interesting facts:

- In the years between 1864 and 1964, 786 million ounces of silver were mined in Idaho; a lot of this silver came from the Coeur d'Alene district.
- In 1964, Idaho's silver was valued at $1.15 billion.

Wild Women

Not all women have to be bad to become notorious. A few wild women stand out in history because they were unconditionally brave, surprisingly unpredictable and unwilling to conform to society's accepted "standards."

These women stand out because they lived in an era when it was uncommon and almost a crime to not obey your husband and do what was expected of them. Two notorious favorites who are well known and famous are May Hutton (an Idaho activist) and Calamity Jane (who often traveled through Idaho). Of the countless women of the Wild West, these two are exceptional, both in their odd ways and in their determination to be who they wanted to be. They broke out of the confines placed on them by society and lived their lives as reckless or as unusual as they wanted.

May Hutton: Inspirational and Adventurous

May Arkwright Hutton (1860–1915) was a notorious leader in the women's suffrage movement. She came to Idaho from Ohio as a young lady, settling in the Coeur d'Alene mining region. She often worked as a cook, barmaid and boardinghouse owner. She gained the title of being the "best cook in the Coeur d'Alenes." Many would have considered her a cheeky and problematic individual for the time.

Just like Calamity Jane, May also liked to dress in men's clothing. She had no problem pulling on a pair of men's overalls and getting down and dirty.

May met her husband-to-be, Levi Hutton (1860–1928), while he was working for the Hercules Mine in northern Idaho, about thirty miles east of Coeur d'Alene. Hutton also did not come from an easy early life. He was born in Iowa and was orphaned at the early age of six. He was not allowed to go to school like other children; instead, he was forced to work on his family's farms. Uneducated and fed up, he left Iowa when he was nineteen years old. He became involved in railroading and found he had a knack for it.

The hardworking pair eventually went from living in a tiny apartment in Wallace to becoming millionaires. A true rags-to-riches team.

May Arkwright Hutton was considered the "best cook in the Coeur d'Alenes!" Later in life, she was an advocate for women's suffrage. *Courtesy of the Library of Congress, item no. 2016863930.*

May's early life also did not start out as an easy one. She was an illegitimate child whose mother died when she was very young. Her father then moved her away to take care of her grandfather. Since he was blind, the job of taking care of him at such a young age must have been extremely difficult. But their relationship was a solid one, filled with love and devotion. Her grandfather loved anything political, and since she had to be his source of travel, she attended his political meetings alongside him.

It was during one of these meetings that the young May was introduced to a man named William McKinley (who would later become the president of the United States). McKinley felt very strongly that women should have the same rights as men. And this idea was planted in the child's head forever. Her grandfather also felt she should never let her plans be limited to what society expected of her.

In 1887, May's life took a turn for the better. After two failed and brief marriages, May finally found the man of her dreams. She was running a boardinghouse in Kellogg, and Hutton frequented the place often, obviously smitten with the young worker. They soon married, moved to Wallace and spent all their savings (a little over $5,000) on a share in the nonproductive Hercules Mine. May also worked at the Wallace Hotel.

The gamble on the Hercules Mine ended up being the best move they ever made, as they made tons of money from their investment. They upgraded from their apartment to a more elaborate two-story Victorian home in Wallace that still stands today at 221 Pine Street.

But even with all her money, the women of Wallace still shunned May. Why? She was considered grossly overweight, at two-hundred-plus pounds (the average woman weighed around one hundred pounds during this time). She dressed obnoxiously (and, obviously, did not wear a corset). She spoke loudly. She was a nonconformist. She was considered uneducated. She worked at a hotel. She got dirty. She helped the miners. She was not the fitting role model the local citizens felt she should be. The list for her being shunned by the local women went on and on.

But instead of getting her feelings hurt, May decided to continue to pursue her passions. She became actively involved in women's rights. She happily entertained elites in her new, larger home in Wallace. She practiced her reading and writing skills until she felt they were eloquent and effective. She was finally starting to be accepted in town.

But 1899 brought troubles to the Huttons and many other individuals involved in the mining business in the Coeur d'Alene Mountains. Trouble and tension had been brewing for years between the hardworking, underpaid miners and their rich bosses. Violence, riots, deaths, explosions, plots to destroy, bribery, robberies, duels, arrests, assault, train take-overs—all these horrible and scandalous events and more were rolled into one big ball of chaos and aggression. When the miners took things a little too far by blowing up the Bunker Hill and Sullivan Mine, all hell broke loose.

Martial law was soon called out, and hundreds of arrests were made. One of the men arrested and taken to the makeshift jail (the converted cow barn called the bullpen) was none other than May's own husband, Levi. The loudmouthed May did not let things rest, and with her constant harassing and pestering, they finally let him go—probably to shut her up.

She continued to practice her writing skills, and she wrote a book titled *The Coeur d'Alenes: Or a Tale of the Modern Inquisition in Idaho.* (She later bought back every copy she could find.)

Letting nothing stand in her way, the bullheaded May ran for the state legislature in 1904. Although she did not win, she became an inspiration to many women with her honor and bravery. Continuing her fight and pledge for women, she joined the National American Woman Suffrage Association and became actively involved in securing women's right to vote.

The years moved on, and May became increasingly involved in the movement. She became the vice-president of the Washington Equal Suffrage Association under the president, Emma DeVoe. She became a huge irritation to Emma in the movement. May was a thorn in her side, as Emma did not like how May carried herself, spoke or worked the field. She felt May threatened their cause.

But May did not diminish their cause; instead, she was able to get the bill through the legislature, finally allowing women to vote in Washington. Next, May was eager to get the irritating Emma replaced by a woman named Mrs. Homer Hill. Yet, Emma could not swallow her pride and immediately began a crusade against May. She formed a group that wasted much time trying to dig up the dirt on May's past. She searched for anything scandalous she could find about May. The group even went so far as to refuse May's yearly dues for her membership. The grounds? They felt she swore too much and had a seedy past.

Apparently, they finally uncovered that when May had been working in the mining camps, she had acquired the nickname Bootleg Mary and run a house of prostitution. It is unclear if May ever really worked as a prostitute, ran a brothel or bootlegged whiskey during her younger years, but the damage had been done to her reputation. Luckily, it didn't stop May.

The Huttons' luck changed, and the couple literally became millionaires overnight with their investment in the Hercules Mine. They built a beautiful mansion in Spokane at 2206 East Seventeenth Avenue that cost $45,000 in 1914 to construct. It was a five-thousand-square-foot grand estate, featuring Mexican mahogany, marble terrazzo flooring, a silver vault and a chauffers' quarters. In the eight years she lived in Spokane, May donated over $450,000 to charity. Levi, outliving her, fulfilled his lifelong dream of building an orphanage. He spent an incredible $750,000 to construct the Hutton Settlement.

Sadly, May only got to enjoy their mansion for a year before dying. The world may never know May's true past, but one thing is certain: she was a shining star in history and deserves to be respected and honored. May died of Bright's disease in 1915 at the early age of fifty-five.

Whether May Hutton was a prostitute turned political activist or not, she certainly was a wild woman from the past.

Calamity Jane: Famous Wild West Woman

One of the most well-known drunken wild women of the West is the famous Calamity Jane (1852–1903), whose real name was Martha Jane Canary Burke. She traveled through the Coeur d'Alene region on her treks back and forth from South Dakota and Montana, on her way to deal Faro in gambling halls in Spokane.

The game Faro was very popular back in the day. It required a board that had the suit of spades glued to it in numerical order. In this game, the aces are low, and the kings are high. The object is to win the most bets, which, back then, were typically one penny. Players would bet that the winning card would be higher than the losing cards by placing their chips. They could bet on the high card (the one on the top of the layout board), one card or several cards. It was a fairly easy game that even drunken men could play.

Calamity Jane was mostly known for hooking up with another Wild West character named Wild Bill Hickok.

Calamity Jane loved to follow the Northern Pacific Railroad routes during her lifetime. While living in Livingston, Montana, she heard the news about a gold rush in Idaho. Around 1884, Jane and eight other girls went to the Coeur d'Alene Mountains through Rathdrum, Kingston and Eagle City, where Calamity Jane began her stage career by telling the interesting and often fabricated story of her wild life. Whiskey went for fifteen cents a shot,

The games of Faro and poker were very popular among the cowboys and soldiers. Calamity Jane loved to deal Faro. *Courtesy of Lee Russel, 1938; from the Library of Congress, item no. 2017781807.*

and Jane (often dressed as a man) was known to boast that she could drink whiskey, chew tobacco and smoke a cigar all at the same time.

Calamity Jane was known to frequent northern Idaho on her many travels and lived in the Coeur d'Alene region briefly in the early 1900s. She had also earned quite the reputation working at a little saloon on Main Avenue in Spokane, which was next to the Owl Saloon.

Some think of Calamity Jane as a common whore. Others think she was nothing more than a drunk following the military and gold/silver mining camps for work. Still others think she sensationalized Wild Bill Hickok's murder in Deadwood, South Dakota—perhaps all are true.

But many believe Calamity Jane was a woman who was simply brave enough to travel thousands of miles alone on horseback, swear often, overdrink daily and dress in men's clothing.

Calamity Jane considered the legendary Will Bill Hickok one of her closest friends, and in 1876, they rode into Deadwood, South Dakota, together (along with many others who were heading that way). Some stories disclose that Hickok barely knew Calamity Jane and preferred to avoid her. Other tales hint that they were lovers.

Opposite: Calamity Jane often traveled through the Coeur d'Alenes in her travels from Deadwood, South Dakota, to Spokane, Washington, and back. *Courtesy of H.R. Locke & Peterson, 1895; from the Library of Congress, item no. 2016649829.*

Above: The table in the bar where Wild Bill Hickok was shot in the back of the head while playing poker. The term "dead man's hand" means that one has two black aces and two black eights. *Courtesy of the author.*

Unfortunately, Wild Bill was shot while playing poker and died soon thereafter—and his Deadwood legend began. The story says that on August 2, Hickok was playing poker in the Nuttal and Mann's Saloon, located at 624 Main Street in Deadwood. A disgruntled man named Jack McCall snuck up behind Hickok and shot him in the back of the head, killing him instantly. He fell to the floor holding a pair of aces and a pair of eights, now known as the "dead man's hand." Although he was acquitted at first, McCall was later found guilty and hanged for the murder. He claimed that he killed Hickok because Hickok had killed his brother in Abilene, Kansas.

Calamity Jane was heartbroken over the loss of her friend and vowed to be buried next to him when it was her time to go. When Calamity Jane died in Terry, South Dakota, on August 1, 1903, her desire to be buried next to

The grave sites of Wild Bill Hickok and Calamity Jane, located in the Mount Moriah Cemetery in Deadwood, South Dakota. *Courtesy of the author.*

Wild Bill Hickok came true. Locals claim it was a joke to bury Calamity Jane next to Hickok, but nevertheless, the two wre buried at Mt. Moriah Cemetery in Deadwood in adjoining grave sites.

So, Wild Bill Hickok and Calamity Jane rest side by side in their graves for all eternity, just as she wished. Hickok really didn't have much say in the matter.

The *Evening Standard*, on May 6, 1911, summed up Calamity when it published: "Men would follow her into any danger. She could handle a rifle, a revolver or knife with the skill of an expert, rode a vicious mustang and seemed utterly without the sense of fear. In short, she was a woman only in sex, a man in mind, heart, muscle and courage."

Calamity Jane was one of the craziest women of the Wild West who will forever be a legend. She would be smiling from her grave if she knew how famous she had become since her death.

2

PROHIBITION, SALOONS AND INTOXICATION

More faceless names fill the Coeur d'Alene newspapers, with advertisements offering the best cigars, the coldest beer, the strongest whiskey, the greatest gambling—and so on.

Proprietor G.E. Reynolds boasted he carried only the finest cigars and smokes in his shop. Coeur d'Alene's Palace Restaurant, run by J.C. Chamberlain (located on the north side of Sherman Avenue between Second and Third Streets), was later run by the duo Moore and Company, which offered excellent oysters and a fine menu.

Over the years, many delightful characters entertained Coeur d'Alene residents and tourists. Bartenders and proprietors who were working in their saloons were eager to pour a nice pint or shot for the ever-thirsty and just-been-paid patrons and soldiers. In 1883, Coeur d'Alene had twenty-six saloons listed in its directory.

Fatty Carroll ran a hussy house and saloon called the Brick House, which tried to please all its patrons in one form or another.

The Transfer Saloon on the corner of Sherman Avenue and Third Street was forever popular and sold Old Crow whiskey by the gallon, with Stephen Whitman bartending. The Exchange Saloon, with Proprietor John Dingwell, had a fun and heavy-handed bartender named Henry Farley to keep the customers happy.

In 1905, there were only thirteen saloons in Coeur d'Alene, but still, no one suffered for the lack of getting a drink in town.

Above: Unidentified men in a typical scene inside a gambling hall around 1910. Many players and saloon owners were robbed during poker and faro games. *Courtesy of the Library of Congress, item no. 2012649628.*

Opposite: During Prohibition, an unidentified woman seated at a soda fountain table is secretly pouring alcohol into a cup from a special cane. *Courtesy of the Library of Congress, item no. 2016832102.*

But the town obviously had sketchy side. Hustlers, gamblers, prostitutes and barkeepers liked to profit from the men who had just gotten paid. Some men were said to go "missing" after getting drunk and visiting a lady for the evening. Others fell into heavy gambling debt, and when they couldn't pay up, their final fate became unknown in Idaho's history. The luckier patrons just woke up with a hangover and empty pockets.

In 1906, the *Coeur d'Alene Evening Press* announced its view on the whole thing, printing, "Prohibition breeds deceit, trickery, sneaking, hypocrisy, political corruption and general contempt for all laws."

In 1911, Coeur d'Alene went dry before its time, as the city council enacted a "dry ordinance."

Coeur d'Alene and the governor of Idaho Moses Alexander signed off and began the process of Prohibition in 1916, and for many locals, this caused great suffering. (Remember, at this time, there was more alcohol

consumed in Idaho than in any other state.) In the neighboring counties, it was recorded that hundreds of saloon owners were in financial distress over the inability to sell alcoholic beverages. Barkeepers tried to satisfy thirsty customers with soda pop, juices and ginger ale, but of course, these beverages did little for the patron who was wishing to get a little drunk. To try to keep patrons entertained, the saloons ramped up their card tables, billiards and cigar selections. They may have even had to hire prettier women to entertain the men.

An unidentified bootlegger was killed in his car while traveling seventy miles per hour to elude Prohibition officers. He was carrying fifty gallons of corn liquor, which was confiscated. *Courtesy of the Library of Congress, item no. 89706543.*

But soon, frustrated people took matters into their own hands, and homemade stills became very popular in the Coeur d'Alene region (and everywhere else). Bootlegging was all the rage, and desperate people began running booze between Idaho and Montana. Rumrunners were bringing booze in from Montana, moonshiners were distilling their own brews and bottle men would hike down mountains with bags of booze to sell locally.

Two local rumrunners, Clarence Reedy and W.A. Rutherford, were known at Wolf Lodge on Lake Coeur d'Alene to be the go-to guys if you needed a fix. Strangely, Rutherford wound up dead on November 17, 1918; he was found beaten to death by an unknown assailant. His pal Reedy was accused and arrested for the murder but was later acquitted due to lack of evidence. The brutal murder of poor Rutherford was never solved.

MOONSHINE MADE HIM CRAZY

On May 30, 1910, the *Coeur d'Alene Press* wrote a story about a man named Al Harris, who was arrested for public drunkenness, as he was acting extremely violent. He was so violent that Chief McGovern had to put him in a padded cell to keep him from hurting himself. It was discovered that he had submitted himself to drinking some homemade moonshine that did not agree with him.

Harris had a decent reputation and had been an employee of the Coeur d'Alene Inn for over four years with no incidents. Yet, after he drank the strange moonshine, he was out of his mind for two days. They continued to hold him in his padded cell. Unfortunately, Harris never seemed to recover and was determined to be forever insane. What was in the moonshine that made the man go crazy—or was something else going on?

Bootlegging in CDA

In the city's crusade against immorality, liquor licenses were being refused to saloon owners, as the councilmembers felt that there was too much "drunkenness and disorderly conduct" in their quaint town. One of the roughest sections of Coeur d'Alene in the early 1900s was termed the Swede Places. In 1905, the Owl Saloon was closed, causing much stress for the owner at the time, Mr. James Cocoran, and the bartender, William Farr. Marshall McGovern felt that the Owl was, by far, the most disorderly saloon in town. Their solution? Daily and nightly raids were a constant irritant to the bar owners, and the punishment was typically a whopping $300 fine and three months in jail. It's hard to stay open for business and pay employees with the inability to sell liquor and having to pay fines like that.

He claimed that the Owl Saloon was promoting drunken orgies, minors participating in the drinking of intoxicating beverages, illegal gambling and improper women in the back part of the building "getting drunk and acting indecent." After much contemplation, Cocoran reluctantly declared he was "powerless" to prevent any orgies.

During Prohibition, government agents would raid saloons, often for no reason. To combat this, proprietors were known to hide whiskey in jugs falsely labeled as gasoline. They would also hide bottles of beer in barrels and label them as Portland cement. This was risky business because if they were caught, their license would immediately be revoked. Two men notoriously beat the streets of Coeur d'Alene in the hopes of catching these criminals: Special Prohibition Officers Sam Cone and Joe Matnyls. If a saloon owner saw these guys coming, you could bet they'd quickly hide the booze.

Even the telephone operators at the Pacific Telephone Company in Coeur d'Alene were in on the game; they would tip off the saloon owners

Eagerly pouring booze into the street was common during Prohibition, as shown by these four in New York City in 1921. Police Commissioner John Leach can be seen to the right; the others are unidentified. *Courtesy of the Library of Congress, item no. 99405169.*

when they heard the officers were going to raid a certain bar. This would give the barkeeps sufficient time to hide or remove any illegal liquor or devices so that they could hopefully keep their licenses.

Chief McGovern had made the first Prohibition arrest in Coeur d'Alene when Richard McWilliams was discovered holding three gallons of red rye whiskey and a gallon of Holland gin while he was staying at the Fernwood Inn in town on his way to Spokane. There was not enough evidence to hold him, even though McGovern produced a slip proving McWilliams had purchased it for Spokane's notorious rumrunner Jimmie Durkin.

Judge Dunn, Sherriff Bailey and his assistants, Adam and Sawyer, were sick to death of these rumrunners and arrested fourteen guilty men. Even the justice of peace in the nearby town of St. Joe was arrested for bootlegging and promoting a gambling device. All were charged with a hefty fine of $200 each.

Prohibition

The problems with whiskey since the late 1700s have always been government control, problems in the community and taxation. As early as George Washington's (1732–1799) presidency, the first of the United States, the government was desperately trying to control alcohol—by taxing it, of course. When the United States got itself in a big financial hurt by pouring tons of money into the Revolutionary War, it chose to tax citizens even more to bail the country out. Nothing has changed over the past two-hundred-plus years. So, the government implemented the Distilled Spirits Tax of 1791.

This new tax did not go over well with saloon owners, farmers or the workers, and the men who were hired to collect these taxes were often savagely beaten and robbed. The problem got so bad that poor old George Washington had to somehow gain control, which he did by

Routine moonshine busts produced many gallons of confiscated illegal liquor. It was tragically believed that the removal of alcohol would clean up the city. *Courtesy of the State Archives of North Carolina, Wikimedia Commons.*

invoking martial law. The local farmers and rebels were no match; they were six hundred workers going against thirteen thousand soldiers.

Luckily, the tax was repealed in the early 1800s by President Jefferson, and business owners were able to make a living again.

During Prohibition, the production and sale of alcohol was considered a felony, and distillers and traffickers could be shot and killed on the spot. But luckily, most officials and police officers loved to drink as well, so they were less stringent and sometimes looked the other way. But the more hard-core officers were relentless, and the refusal of liquor licenses forced bar owners to devise a different way of selling alcohol. Thus, bootlegging became popular sport during Prohibition. Bootlegging was the illegal manufacturing, transportation and sale of anything intoxicating in nature. Many citizens felt that by prohibiting the sale (and thus the drinking) of booze, many folks would be forced to clean up their act and save money.

It didn't work very well.

The folks in Coeur d'Alene, Spokane and northern Idaho were not happy in general, nor were they happy with one another. Arrests that later led to appeals and even more problems were not unheard of. Lawyers argued that bootleggers and distillers worked for the good of the community, and opposing lawyers argued it was appropriate to collect taxes on booze. Cases were argued and thrown out. A local United States district attorney named Hoyt Ray led a campaign in Idaho that became known as the North Idaho Whiskey Rebellion in the 1930s.

As for the locals, they thought there should have been more rebellions.

The Bootlegging Hendershot

One of Coeur d'Alene's finest troublemakers was a man named William Hendershot. In 1908, Hendershot ran the Hendershot Hotel, which quickly became a seedy house of ill repute. His hotel was located next to the post office in town. The following year, Hendershot and his wife were denied their liquor license. This complication forced them to only sell soft drinks, which didn't produce much profit. What were they to do?

The next year, the Hendershots were still not abiding by the law. Mr. Hendershot was charged (again) with bootlegging. He just couldn't seem to stay out of trouble. In a stupid attempt to be found not guilty, Hendershot and his partner in crime, Reilly Roby (also charged), decided to come up with a scheme. They cornered F.A. Dillon, who worked for the Swain Detective

An unidentified police officer investigating a wrecked car loaded with cases of moonshine in 1922. *Courtesy of the Library of Congress, item no. 89709481.*

Agency, and offered him money in exchange for lying on the witness stand. They begged him to tell the jury that they were in Coeur d'Alene during that time and not off selling illegal booze elsewhere.

But Detective Dillon had a plan of his own. He rented rooms at the Carlyle Hotel and asked the men to meet him there. At the Carlyle, Dillon and his coworker James Beavers planned to trap the guilty men. The other detectives, who were renting the room next door, would listen through the walls as Hendershot and Roby tried to bribe the detectives. The plan worked. They offered the investigators $150 each to lie about their whereabouts. They agreed to all meet later at the Lakeview Bar to collect their money, and Dillon and Beavers agreed to the payout.

Later that night, the men met at the Lakeview Bar as planned, and the $300 was handed out to the men in gold coins. Then the confident bootleggers exited the bar and walked down Sherman Avenue, toward the Hotel Idaho, but the men were quickly cut off by other officers when they confidently entered Hotel Idaho's bar. Deputy Sheriff Adams handcuffed Roby, but the wiry Hendershot took off running and scooted out the back door of the bar. He hailed a taxi without delay and was off to Spokane and the safety of the border of Washington State.

The Prohibition Cowboy: Al "Scarface" Capone's Secret Brother

A handsome and rugged hero whom the local press called "Two Gun Hart" and the "Beau of the Coeur d'Alenes" was actually the secret brother of the notorious Chicago gang leader Al "Scarface" Capone. The brothers ran on opposite sides of the law, and Two Gun Hart (whose real name was James Vincenzo Capone, but local people knew him as Richard J. Hart) felt it would be best if he hid his true identity from the world.

Hart's concocted story was that he came from Oklahoma on a train, seeking adventure. He got off the train in a little town called Emerson, Nebraska. There, he became a local hero by rescuing a young girl named Margaret and her family from the river during a flood. The teenage daughter of the family, Kathleen Winch, fell instantly in love with the brave man, and they were married. He then became the marshal of Homer, Nebraska. He told tales of being a soldier, circus traveler, horse trainer, bounty hunter, police officer, cowboy, champion wrestler and a sure shot—most were true. He gained a reputation for being a well-dressed man, always wearing impeccable clothing and a white ten-gallon hat. It was rumored he would often change his clothes three or four times a day, and he wanted to dress like his two favorite Hollywood actors of the era, Bill Hart and Tom Mix.

In 1919, the Eighteenth Amendment to the Constitution was changed to "prohibit the manufacturing and sale of intoxicating liquors." Then, in October that same year, Congress passed the Volstead Act, which allowed the law to actually be enforced, so the demand for Prohibition agents was at an all-time high.

Hart felt he fit the bill, applied for the position and was quickly hired. During his career as a Prohibition agent, Hart arrested hundreds of bootleggers and moonshiners. Hart was adventurous and rugged and would travel via horseback (on his horse named Buckskin Betty), automobile, snowshoes or skis—whatever it took to pursue and catch his criminal. His record tallied the capture of over twenty murderers and countless arrests. He became a legendary hero to local citizens and a much-hated predicament to bootleggers and moonshiners. He would dress in various costumes to portray the image of a common working man or drunk in order to get leads on who was making and selling illegal booze.

But in 1923, Hart's luck changed for the worse. While he and a few other men were chasing a criminal named Ed Morvace in Sioux City, Nebraska,

Two-Gun Hart would travel on his horse Buckskin Betty or by car, snowshoes or skis to catch criminals. He captured more than twenty murderers and made countless arrests. *Courtesy of the Library of Congress, item no. 200271600 9; photographer, Erwin E. Smith.*

a bullet struck Morvace in the back of his neck, exiting through his mouth; this killed the young family man instantly. Instead of being grateful that the criminal was caught, the locals were outraged, and Hart began receiving death threats. Over the next few years, the Hart family traveled from state to state—Nebraska, Wyoming, Idaho and Washington—to escape the ridicule.

Three years later, in 1926, Hart made a comeback and became a special agent for the Bureau of Indian Affairs in South Dakota. The following year brought Hart some more glory, as he was appointed the personal bodyguard of President Calvin Coolidge while he was visiting the Black Hills in South Dakota.

But Hart and his family ventured back to Idaho when he was transferred to the Spokane Indian Reservation to work again as an agent.

In 1928, the *Spokane Chronicle* worried about Hart's disappearance, fearing he met with foul play, but Hart was alive and well. He was busy in Spokane, working at the federal building there. At one time, he even arrested the manager of the famous Davenport Hotel for the illegal sale of liquor. Next, Hart arrested the manager of Spokane's Ritter's Drugstore on Second and Washington Streets for passing a bad check and selling denatured alcohol as an intoxicant.

In 1929, Hart was back in the law game in the Coeur d'Alene Mountains, his beat covering two hundred square miles, overseeing almost one thousand Natives. The Natives had great respect for Hart and called him the "Great White Father." The Hart family moved from home to home while living in Coeur d'Alene.

Once, while he worked as a Prohibition agent, Hart pursued a heavily armed local Native named Charles Cherrapin, who was guilty of killing his wife on the Coeur d'Alene Indian Reservation. Cherrapin was a well-educated and very well-respected wheat farmer on reservation. Unfortunately, Cherrapin's wife had run off with another man, and he told everyone who would listen that if she ever tried to return to him, he would kill her. Well, when she did try to return to Cherrapin, he kept his promise and put four bullets in her. She should have listened to his warning. Cherrapin quickly left town heavily armed and tried to run from the police, but he was no match for Hart, who had a gleaming reputation for being able to locate men on the plains with his great tracking skills. When Cherrapin discovered that sharpshooter Hart was the officer after him, he knew he didn't have a chance and quickly surrendered. Cherrapin was tried in Coeur d'Alene, where he received a guilty verdict for second-degree murder and was sentenced to ten years in jail.

The following year, Hart confronted another Native man who was wanted by the police. During their scuttle, Hart shot and killed the man. Although he was acquitted of any wrongdoing with the crime, the commissioner of Indian affairs was angered and promptly fired Hart.

From 1931 to 1935, Hart was employed as a range detective until he was reinstated as an Indian agent. The job did not last long, as Hart longed to be back in Nebraska. So, the Harts returned to Homer, Nebraska, where Hart became a justice of the peace.

In 1935, Hart faced another career challenge. A group of men, out for revenge (one of their family members had been killed by Two Gun Hart), cornered him and proceeded to beat him up. One of the thugs used a pair of brass knuckles, which ultimately cost Hart the loss of his vision in one eye. After that episode, Hart's once-exciting life took a quick downward spiral. He was soon broke and unhappy.

The Great Depression was in full swing, and millions suffered. Hart and his family were among them. He made a pittance for a wage, and it was rumored that he had to steal food just to feed his family. (Hart's son Harry later told reporters that his father never stole a thing in his life.)

But during the early 1950s, Special Agent Hart was back to working in Idaho. Yet again, he longed for home, and the Harts returned to Homer, Nebraska—the very place his travels had led him from decades earlier. He always felt that Homer was his real home.

Hart died of a heart attack at the age of sixty on October 1, 1952, in his favorite little hometown of Homer.

And now, the true story of Richard J. Hart's life:

Although most of the preceding facts are true, Hart kept most of his family history and crime connections to himself. There are many conflicting stories, facts, dates and details for Hart's complicated life.

Hart's real name was James Vincenzo Capone. He did not come from Oklahoma, but from Italy, where he was born in 1892. His family came to New York and settled in Brooklyn before his brother Alphonse was born. His parents, Gabriele and Teresina Capone, were eager to live a good life in America.

Later, the four young brothers—Alphonse, Raffaele, Salvatore and Vincenzo—banded together to form a ruthless street gang. It was a matter of survival. Vincenzo decided to Americanize his name, so he chose to be called James instead.

The famous Al Capone (Alphonse) received his facial scars (the reason acquired the nickname "Scarface") sometime during a brutal fight with another gang in Brooklyn. This discouraged Vincenzo, who quickly decided the gangster life was not for him, and he fled New York to be on his own and to make a new life for himself. When little Al was just eight years old, his older brother Vincenzo left the family and joined a circus gig called the Miller Brothers Ranch Wild West Show. During this time, Vincenzo renamed himself again after his movie star idol, William S. Hart.

After he created a fictitious past for himself and distanced himself from his New York family, Hart lived his life as a proud husband and officer of the law. He really only learned about his now-famous brother's mobster dealings through the headlines he read in the newspapers. His younger brother (now an adult) Al was termed "Public Enemy no. 1" by the press. Al was the head boss of the ruthless gang called the Chicago Outfit and became one of the most feared mobsters in recorded history.

By the 1920s, Al "Scarface" had become a multimillionaire by operating brothels and gambling halls and running illegal booze. He also made his millions through bribery, murder and torture—things the older Capone could live without. Headline after headline appeared, with the famous Al Capone being written up for one crime after another. Hart turned a blind

Al Capone's mugshot from 1931. Although he and his brother were on opposite sides of the law, they agreed to stay out of each other's territories. *Courtesy of the U.S. federal government, public domain.*

eye to his notorious brother's violent criminal behavior and just lived his own life.

But when a complicated bank heist occurred at the Lincoln National Bank in Lincoln, Nebraska, in 1930, Hart became suspicious that his brother and his gang had something to do with it. The six robbers got away with $2.7 million in cash and bonds (about $32 million today). The irritated Hart demanded that Al's gang return the money and bonds to the bank. Al calmly told his brother that the Lincoln bank heist had nothing to do with him or his gang but that he knew who had pulled it off. With Hart's demand and Al's influence, the bank robbers returned the stolen currency, and the relieved Lincoln depositors got their money back.

Around that time, Al's luck ran out, and he was headed to prison for tax evasion—so was his brother Ralph.

Hart continued to live his life as an officer and agent, but when he eventually fell on hard times, he decided to humbly ask his brothers for money. They eagerly gave Hart a check to help him and his family out.

In 1937, Al Capone was sent to Alcatraz Prison in San Francisco, California, but was released in 1939 due to poor health. Al had been diagnosed years earlier with syphilis, and his health was deteriorating rapidly. Ralph had been released from jail before Al. Once both brothers were out of jail, they all gathered at the grand Capone estate in Mercer, Wisconsin, where they would often meet to spend time as a family.

Soon, Ralph began laundering money through his brother James (also known as Hart). But the IRS caught up with the brothers, and the real truth about Hart's connection with the famous Capone Gang finally became public. Hart took the fall for his brothers and never faltered on the witness stand.

The Capone brothers were definitely in deep water with tax evasion charges, among many others. But despite all their troubles, the brothers and family remained close.

Vincenzo, or Hart, died of a heart attack in October 1952 and was buried at the Omaha Valley Cemetery in Homer, Nebraska. His headstone reads "Richard J. Hart," not his real name.

The famous Al Capone died on a cold day in Florida in January 1947 at just forty-eight years old after suffering complications with a stroke and

The Capone family hideout in Wisconsin, where Al and James spent time together. Al's men smuggled liquor from Canada to the private hideout. *Courtesy of the Library of Congress, item no. 2011633665; photographer, Carol M. Highsmith.*

cardiac arrest. His mental ability had deteriorated to that of a twelve-year-old due to his syphilis. He was originally buried in Chicago, and then his body was moved to Illinois, his final resting place. His gravestone simply states, "Alphonse Capone, 1899–1947, My Jesus Mercy."

The two brothers were as different as can be—on opposite sides of the law—but their brotherly love never failed in the end.

Homemade Whiskey

Prohibition seemed like a good idea to many people because they thought it would help families out financially, as men would not be wasting their paychecks on booze. In fact, most Idahoans voted in favor of the new law. But just because a law was passed prohibiting the consumption of alcohol, that did not mean the public was actually going to stop drinking.

The process of home brewing became a big sport and moneymaker for thousands of people. The process was fairly simple but could be dangerous if done improperly. Moonshiners would create a mash by mixing whatever grain they chose with a fermenter (either yeast or sugar) and water. This would sit for a couple of weeks until the product turned

Four unidentified police officers proudly stand next to the largest whiskey still ever confiscated during Prohibition (1922). *Courtesy of the Library of Congress, item no. 91796643.*

to alcohol. Then they would heat the mash mix over medium heat so that the alcohol would rise up through the condenser and drip back down into a collection pot. This would then be filtered. Most stills were made from copper. The moonshine would then be sold discreetly to buyers, and hopefully, the person making it would not be caught and arrested.

Opium Dens and Delirium

Opium was a big business, making tons of money for lots of people. It was smuggled into the United States from China in much the same way it is still being smuggled in today. Opium is a drug that is made by cutting the capsule (seed pod) of a beautiful red opium poppy at sunrise. The sap that bleeds out is then dried, scraped off and saved. The problem of opium smuggling became so bad that, in 1881, a treaty was formed between the United States and China that had a crystal-clear clause prohibiting the Chinese from importing opium into the United States for any reason. What other reasons (aside from drug use) opium would be imported for are a mystery.

In 1893, opium was being sold for $10.50 per pound. It took a lot of poppy sap to create a pound of opium. Even though opium was not supposed to be entering the country, it still came in boat loads—literally. Much to the local authorities' dismay, opium continued to be smuggled into America in record-breaking numbers in the years 1893 and 1894.

During the 1890s, a Chinese man named Gee Dong was a big-time opium dealer in Coeur d'Alene. He was getting his supply through a port in Oakland, California, and it was transported by ship from British Columbia. Dong was originally a laundryman, but he quickly realized that dealing opium made him a lot more money than cleaning clothes. His smugglers would sneak the drugs into the port on the coal-laden ships that came to unload in Oakland. Since inspectors only worked during the day, it was an easy task for them to commit these crimes. The ships going to San Francisco could easily hide drugs among the milk containers and vegetables. The confident Dong was proud of himself when he was able to unload a $10,000 shipment of opium at the wharf in Coeur d'Alene (off Franklin Street), right in front of the officers' eyes, without getting caught. For his trouble, Dong got to keep two of the boxes full of opium. The captain of the ship, "Pete," lived in Seattle, Washington, but came to the port in Coeur d'Alene often. He probably got to keep a box or two of the drugs as payoff.

Two unidentified men get high on opium in a Chinese den, similar to the ones located in Coeur d'Alene during the early 1900s. *Courtesy of the Library of Congress, item no. 2012648354.*

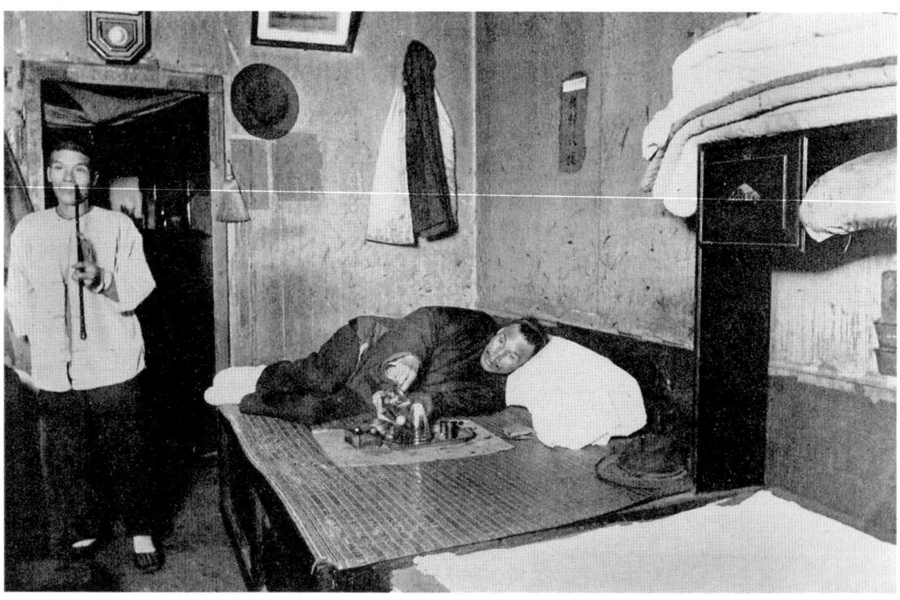

Opium business owners Lou Sunn and Jo Sing's den was located behind the Hotel Idaho in 1907. When they were arrested, they chose to go to Spokane instead of serving jail time. *Courtesy of Wellcome M0018554, Wikimedia Commons,* Unidentified Men in an Opium Den in San Francisco.

In 1907, Coeur d'Alene had its fair share of the opium market and several opium dens. One spring, two city night watchmen named Earl Sanders and Frank Huyck raided an opium joint they had been informed of. It was located in the back of a Chinese laundry business that was situated behind the Hotel Idaho. Sanders and Huyck were standing watch in front of the Coeur d'Alene Bank when they noticed some men walking into the Chinese laundry and not coming back out. When they asked a man nearby if he knew anything about it, the stranger told the officers that the Chinese laundry storefront was just a ruse for the opium den in the back.

The officers quickly charged into the business, where they could immediately smell an odd odor. In the back, they caught two White men stoned off their gourd; they were so high on opium that they barely noticed they were being arrested. There were two Chinese men working the joint, Lou Sunn and Jo Sing, who were also arrested. They were told to leave Coeur d'Alene immediately, which they did. They boarded the next train headed to Spokane.

In November 1906, the *Coeur d'Alene Press* announced the new Chinese opium regulation and demanded that "all teachers, scholars, soldiers and sailors would be given three months to kick the habit!"

The *Coeur d'Alene Press* told of a raid conducted by Chief McGovern in June 1908 that left two more men arrested for smoking opium. George Stewart and W.W. Howard were found high on a houseboat near the Northern Pacific Dock; the houseboat's only purpose was for those who were seeking to get loaded in privacy. Both men were taken to jail with a $100 bond each, but once the men were released, they never appeared for their trial and were never seen again in Coeur d'Alene.

Coeur d'Alene's Bad Man: Fatty Carroll

Coeur d'Alene was a very seedy town in its early days. It was considered one of the roughest towns between Portland and Saint Paul. One of the most feared men of those days was Jim Metzger, also known as Fatty Carroll. Carroll owned seventy acres on the Coeur d'Alene River, and he was feared by everyone—and for good reason.

The *Coeur d'Alene Press* described Carroll best on November 23, 1897, when it printed, "Jim Metzger, known as Fatty Carroll, Coeur d'Alene's bad man, has a graveyard of his own near town." That year, Carroll found himself in front of Judge Will on an assault and battery charge that was brought up by a shoemaker named Bade Grundt, who leased a section of his building. Perhaps Grundt chickened out or was threatened by Carroll, but either way, he requested the charges be dropped and the case dismissed, so no conviction ever occurred.

Fatty Carroll's dance hall was considered the most popular spot around in the 1880s. People claimed it was absolutely one of the toughest joints in Coeur d'Alene's history.

Another of Carrol's places was called the Variety Saloon; it was opened in 1887, and in 1897, it became a gambling resort called Bonanza City, where Faro cards and plenty of poker games ensued. No one crossed Fatty. If they did, they might end up in a shallow grave somewhere, never to be found. Legend is that Fatty had a house he built over the river, and if he invited you to this place, you were sure to be killed. There was supposedly a trapdoor that was conveniently situated over the river.

Fatty also owned a brothel on the corner of Fourth Street and Sherman Avenue in Coeur d'Alene. Later, when workers were prepping the ground for a foundation for the new Wilson's Pharmacy, several skeletons were found in shallow graves. These were thought to be the Natives and three soldiers who went missing from Fort Sherman in 1887. That same year, one of Fatty's buildings caught fire, and two men lost their lives: Lottie Haines, who was sleeping, burned to death; and "Uncle" John died while trying to retrieve his personal belongings from the building.

In the early 1900s, more skeletons were found near Tubbs Hill, where Carroll's Variety once was. When the Coeur d'Alene and Spokane Railway Company was excavating the car barn, workers found multiple skeletons buried beneath a few feet of soil. These were also thought to be the remains of the missing soldiers, since it was very near Fort Sherman.

In the years between 1901 and 1903, four more sets of bones were discovered. The first were found at the Coeur d'Alene Lumber Company (the old site of the Opera House). Excavators dug up a partial skull, jaw, ribs and a few larger bones. Rumor said that these skeletons were the product of Fatty's terror, as he was also called the "king of the community." The discovery of these bones was recorded in the *Coeur d'Alene Press* on June 1, 1901, in an article called "They Dug up Human Bones."

Fatty sold his seventy-acre parcel to the Fort Sherman Lumber Company for the development of a sawmill in 1902. The mill was to be built on an old flat where the Riverside Saloon sat.

Another set of bones was found in a box at what was termed Dr. Scallon's Block, located on the corner of Fourth Street and Sherman Avenue, which is where Fatty owned the brothel that later became the Wilson's Drugstore.

In 1903, the third set of bodies was discovered between Mullan Road and Fort Sherman. Interestingly, even in 2018, construction workers unearthed more human remains at the block of Mullan Avenue. Who do those bones belong to? Did all of these unfortunate victims die at the hand of the terrible Fatty Carroll? Others state strongly that no bones have ever been found, but newspaper articles state otherwise.

Fatty was no stranger to crime. In 1903, he was charged with disorderly conduct when he tangled with a man named John Garton at the Crystal Saloon, located at the corner of Main Avenue and Division Street. Garton kicked Fatty in the face while he was down on the ground. There are no records of Fatty ever going to prison for any crimes or any murders. Was Fatty above the law—did even the police fear him?

Disappearing Coeur d'Alene Soldiers

Early Coeur d'Alene was troubled by criminals and murderers, and many were living and working in plain sight. Dozens of incidences of foul play, robberies and assaults were recorded in local papers each week. As for shallow graves, some still insist that no bones have ever been found beneath the surface of old Coeur d'Alene, but that would be extremely hard to imagine when there has been so much recorded in the press.

When more skeletons were discovered in 1903 by workers who were excavating a roadway for the Spokane and Coeur d'Alene Electric Line, many wondered if they were the bodies of the missing soldiers they had read about.

Another area that was being excavated was the site of a former saloon called O'Reilly's, run by Ed O'Reilly, a former soldier himself. O'Reilly also owned the oldest Coeur d'Alene saloon, the Car Barn.

During its heyday, soldiers were lured to O'Reilly's on payday to partake in gambling, drinking and the comfort of women. Many never returned to their posts the next morning and were presumably "deserters" of the army, so no follow-up investigations were ever conducted by the military police. It is interesting that soldiers could simply disappear without an investigation.

O'Reilly's was originally built in 1886 and featured a saloon out front and a backroom where women would entertain guests. The O'Reilly Saloon continued to operate until it burned down in 1893. This backlot section is where the bodies were found in 1903. It was believed that the soldiers were murdered in cold blood for the mere amounts of their paychecks.

In 1891, the *Kootenai Herald* listed saloon license bonds, and the name "O'Reilly & White" appears, so the story holds true that there was probably a saloon there. O'Reilly did not have the best reputation in town, and he was eventually run out of Coeur d'Alene by the locals. Did the murderous spree end after he left town?

Fort Sherman and a Crazy Soldier

Fort Sherman continued to have its share of troubles. In 1893–94, three men's lives were changed forever. The tragic chain of events began when Private Joseph Roberts shot and killed O'Leary of the United States Army at Fort Sherman in the summer of 1893. The two had become entangled in an argument; Roberts was extremely jealous of O'Leary because he had been passed over for a promotion that was given to O'Leary.

The argument escalated until Roberts aimed his revolver at O'Leary and pulled the trigger. O'Leary could not be saved and died. A warrant was issued for the arrest of Roberts on June 20. Roberts proceeded to try to commit suicide multiple times and was eventually judged insane. He was eventually moved to a jail in Moscow while awaiting his trial and legal proceedings.

In 1834, Congress passed a law to "act to regulate trade and intercourse with the Indian tribes and to preserve peace on the frontiers." In 1847, the punishment for violating this act escalated to include prison time, not just a fine. Then, in 1892, the sentence increased to up to two years in prison and a $300 fine for each offense.

The tragic outcome of a third man comes into play in 1894, when a young teenage boy named John Witte was caught selling liquor to Natives on the Coeur d'Alene Reservation. Unfortunately for Witte, he had been caught selling the booze red-handed and was spending time in prison in Moscow.

Sheriff J.L. Naylor knew that his prisoner and former soldier Roberts was mentally unstable and dangerous. Naylor had tried in vain to get the dangerous and unpredictable Roberts moved from the prison to an insane asylum for a long time. Yet, for some odd reason, Witte and Roberts developed an unusual friendship, and when Witte became ill, Roberts tenderly cared for him.

But a strange and grisly twist soon occurred between the men.

One Monday night, Deputy Donahue was making his rounds and locking up the prisoners in their cells for the evening. As he passed Witte's cell, he noticed the boy was already sleeping in his bed, so he just closed the door and locked it up, moving on to the next prisoner's cell. In the morning, when Marshall Crutcher arrived at work, he received the orders to finally move Roberts out of prison and on to the appointed insane asylum. But the order was received one day too late.

When the door to Witte's cell was opened by the guard that morning, Witte was still asleep—or so it seemed. When the officer approached Witte to prod him to get up, he noticed that the sleeping boy was nothing more than a bundle of sheets! The first thought in the officer's mind was that Witte had somehow managed to escape the prison.

If only that were true.

The ghastly reality was that Witte had been brutally murdered the night before. The boy's body was found wrapped in blankets and shoved behind a large trunk in his cell.

Since Roberts was crazy, he was an immediate suspect, regardless of the friendly kinship that had developed between himself and Witte. When they questioned Roberts about Witte, he calmly said, "A miracle was performed after an understanding between myself, Witte and Almighty God." He claimed that after he spoke to God, it was decided that Witte should be killed. Apparently, Roberts administered the skull-crushing blow after Witte had fallen asleep. It was discovered later that Roberts had used a cast-iron stove lid to carry out the horrific deed. Roberts claimed he had used an axe, but no axe was ever found on the site.

Coroner Friedline reported that the poor boy had suffered a terrible assault and that his skull had been crushed, causing instant death. For some unexplained reason, Roberts continued to violate the boy's body, slashing him with a dull knife over forty-five times.

Witte's remains were buried in the Moscow Cemetery in a potters' field late that October.

Three men were brought together in an odd way, and the tragic result was the senseless murders of two innocent men by the hands of one angry and insane man.

Drinking, Stabbing and Peeling Potatoes

One tragic story of how alcohol can destroy lives (which is why some felt Prohibition was a cure for the problems caused by intoxication) is the unfortunate story of a murder committed in 1936 by a drunken woman named Lucy Anasta.

The twenty-three-year-old stabbed her younger sister Christine in an alcohol-induced fight on the Coeur d'Alene Indian Reservation. It became a well-publicized four-day-long trial.

The night before the murder, Lucy and her sister had been at their stepdad Peter Frank's house, drinking. The next morning, the girls were still partying. The tragic day began as they girls continued drinking some home-brewed whiskey while making breakfast. One thing led to another, and the girls began fighting. Christine wanted more alcohol. The argument moved outside, and soon, a bloody Christine came back into the house, dazed. She muttered, "I have been cut. Lucy cut me!"

Lucy had stabbed Christine with the paring knife she had been using to peel potatoes. The stab wound stuck between her ribs and caused a hemorrhage. Christine died on the couch while waiting for help. Soon, Lucy was arrested and taken to jail.

The trial lasted four days and caused quite a sensation. Lucy wore a blue jacket and brown skirt and appeared calm. The jury felt compassion for Lucy, as she only weighed eighty-five pounds and had a deformed back. E.H. Casterlain, the council for Christine, argued that if Lucy was strong enough to break Christine's grasp of the knife, she was "strong enough to have thrust the knife into Christine's heart!"

E.T. Knudson, who represented Lucy, argued back, "The girls loved one another, and Lucy tried to watch over Christine, who sometimes drank too much." Lucy was acquitted of the crime.

When Eva Campbell, the stepdad's wife, was asked about the drunken confrontation that led to Christine's murder, she oddly chimed in, "The girls did not do a very good job of peeling the potatoes."

A Long Night at the Spokane Bar in Coeur d'Alene

Another brutal ending linked to drunkenness came in November 1906; it was the untimely death of Malcolm Coombs by the hands of Lee Garrett, a boy of about twenty years of age.

On that long, cold night in Coeur d'Alene, Lee Garrett was already drunk and harassing another patron at the bar when Coombs entered with a friend named Jack Carlisle, the bartender at the nearby Silver Grill. They were just there for a friendly beer together, nothing more. After a while, Coombs got tired of listening to Garrett antagonize the old rancher and joked, "If you want to fight someone, then step outside."

All three men walked out the back door of the bar. Carlisle thought they were all just playing around, so he went back inside. Coombs said to Garrett, "You are going too far for me," and turned to make his way back into the bar. As he moved away, Garrett quickly stabbed Coombs two times in the heart with a long knife.

The startled Coombs went back inside grabbed a fireplace poker and went out and hit Garrett on the head a couple of times. Then he went back inside and said to his pal Carlisle, "I'm stabbed, Jack! I am all cut to pieces." Coombs then fell to the floor. The men carried him to the back of the bar and laid him down on a mattress.

Unknowingly, he had fractured Garrett's skull in two places with the poker.

Coombs quietly died from his wounds. Undertaker G. Arthur Goble was summoned, and he came to the Spokane Bar to remove Coombs body to take it back to his mortuary on Coeur d'Alene Street.

The *Coeur d'Alene Press* reported on November 21 that after the fight, the drunken Garrett had walked over to the Silver Grill covered in blood, the knife still clasped in his red-stained hand. He belligerently yelled to the patrons in the bar, "He cut me, the ——! Give me a gun, and I'll kill him! Let me finish him!" He did not know that Coombs was already dead.

Garrett was quickly arrested by night watchman Carl Kronblandt. He was taken to the hospital for his head wounds; the doctor examined him and gave him a shot of morphine for the pain. Garrett was diagnosed as suffering from a compound fracture to his skull.

After Garrett was put in jail, he became extremely anxious and nervous, and he began acting very strangely. He would grab the guards' sleeves as they passed, begging for them not to leave him alone. Perhaps Garrett's behavior was brought on by the upcoming trial (surely to result in him hanging until his death), or perhaps it was due to the brain injury inflicted by his skull fractures.

Garrett's attorney argued that the killing was done in self-defense. The state countered that Garrett had stabbed Coombs prior to receiving the head wound, so it could not have been in self-defense. Judge Woods didn't have much sympathy and sentenced Garrett to thirty years in jail, stating that if Garrett was not just a young man, he would have sentenced him to life in prison.

Garrett eventually ended up in the insane ward in the jail at Rathdrum.

Coombs was a well-liked and hardworking man. He was thirty-five years old at the time of his death and had been hired as a brakeman for the Coeur d'Alene and Spokane Railway.

3

PISTOLS, PROBLEMS AND VIOLENCE

Violence is a part of any community, and early Idaho sure had its fair share of problems. Almost everyone, even the women, carried a gun, and they were not afraid to use them. The Idaho State Penitentiary alone housed over twenty female inmates convicted for murder in the late 1800s. Unsolved murders and gun violence persisted in the area, and several bodies were found over the years, floating in Lake Coeur d'Alene with gunshot wounds to the head.

Early Kootenai County had a very small population of White people, and the Northern Pacific Railroad brought in hundreds of laborers of all nationalities. In 1882, the area was still a wild and unsettled region. In 1880, the population of Kootenai County was a mere 318, but in 1884, it jumped to over 2,000. In 1889, when violence rang through the world, the brave men of Kootenai County were eager to go to war to help liberate Cuba. Of the 51 men of Company B who left on May 12, 1889, 21 of them were residents from Coeur d'Alene. When the battered men returned from the war on October 2, 1899, they received a very warm welcome from hundreds of Spokane, Coeur d'Alene and other nearby residents. A speech was provided by C.L. Heitman from the balcony of the Coeur d'Alene Inn, and a lavish banquet was provided for the soldiers.

Many men took the matters of law into their own hands, impatient with legal proceedings and the outlandish ratio of criminals to policemen. They saw no offense in the public taking justice into their own hands by whatever means necessary.

An Unsolved Lynching

One of the most horrendous crimes in north Idaho occurred in 1885.

An early pioneer named David M. Fraser typically worked alone in his shop, the Fraser General Store, and then slept in the back of his building. In the morning, he would predictably meet friends for breakfast and coffee at the town café—but not on the morning of the New Year in 1885.

When he failed to arrive for breakfast, Fraser's friends became worried and walked to his store to see if he was alright. What they discovered were his grisly remains lying on the blood-soaked floor by the front door. A long trail of blood led all the way from the backroom where he had slept. If the poor man had cried out, no one would have heard him anyway, as the racket of the fireworks during the celebration that night would had concealed any sounds of a struggle.

The wickedness and viciousness of the murder was unthinkable to his friends.

Fraser was violently hacked to pieces by the use of multiple weapons. His body suffered numerous wounds caused by the use of an axe, a hatchet and a knife. And then, just to make sure he was actually dead, the perpetrators also stuck a gun in the poor man's mouth and pulled the trigger.

Once the news spread through the small town, everyone was shocked.

Who in their tiny community would commit such a heinous sin against one of their own? Investigators soon came to the crime scene, hoping to discover clues as to who the murderers were. Local citizens also surveyed the shop in the hopes of finding clues. After much checking around with the locals, police discovered several possibilities as to why the man was killed.

1. Fraser, although well liked, was unwanted by some Chinese locals because he was one of the few White merchants in town. Apparently, several of the three hundred local Chinese wished for him (and his store) to be gone.
2. More rumors came about that said Fraser had tipped off the Natives that some Chinese men had been ripping them off, paying them with fake gold dust for their vegetables and products.
3. The store's safe had been tampered with. Was robbery the motive?

The sheriff was desperate to catch the criminals. Finally, five Chinese men were taken into custody and questioned. They would not talk. Even without any hard evidence, the Chinese men were implicated in the murder and charged with the crime.

Eager for a confession, the police had a young man named Lon Sears (who understood the Chinese language) dress up and pretend to be a drunken Native. They tossed him in the same cell as the Chinese men. As Sears laid on the floor, pretending to be in an alcoholic stupor, he overheard the detained Chinese men discussing what they could do to not be charged with the murder.

After this evidence was obtained, the five went to trial for the coldblooded murder of Fraser. The sheriff decided to move the prisoners to the nearby town of Murray, where the county courthouse was located. On the way there, a large team of masked men aggressively approached the group of men. The sheriff's posse was soon overpowered by the unknown bandits. The assailants quickly threw long ropes over some nearby big trees and proceeded to hang the

Hanging or lynching was a popular way of getting justice for victims of crimes, as seen with this crowd that witnessed the execution of Lincoln's assassins. *Courtesy of Alexander Gardner, public domain, Wikimedia Commons.*

prisoners one by one as the lawmen stood by, unable to do anything for fear of being lynched along with the Chinese men.

This area became known as Hangman's Creek.

The masked bandits who decided to take the law into their own hands were never identified, captured or charged with the brutal hangings. The Chinese authorities demanded another formal investigation, but nothing ever came of it. This decision would eventually cost the United States government $25,000 in reparations, since the Chinese men never received a fair trial.

In sadness, the local friends of the Chinese men who were killed paid a man named Bill Curry $250 to cut the hanged men down from the trees and move their bodies four miles away to a camp to be properly buried.

In 1913, three Chinese men traveled all the way from San Francisco, California, to retrieve the bodies of the men who had died in the Coeur d'Alene Mountains. In all, a total of nine bodies were selectively exhumed and their bones placed carefully in boxes to travel back to San Francisco. Five sets of bones were shipped to the Duck Lee Company, and another four Chinese men who had died in 1860 were sent to Wang Hong Company.

THE CHICKEN RANCH MURDER

A brutal murder was committed between two supposed friends in December 1909, and eventually, the killer was sentenced to be hanged in Coeur d'Alene on May 20, 1910. The story begins when two workmates, twenty-three-year-old Fred Gruber (also called Fred George or Carlisle) and fifty-year-old John H. Billings, worked together as employees of the Parker Carnival Company. After the summer of tent shows was over, Gruber grudgingly realized that he hadn't saved any of his earnings, but the financially careful Billings had.

Frustrated over his financial dilemma, Gruber devised a plan to rob Billings. He lured Billings to Coeur d'Alene on the pretense of going to see a chicken ranch that was for sale; he said they could be partners in the business together. Billings thought this might be a good plan, so he went along with it.

That night, the pair stayed at the Inn Hotel. In the morning, they had breakfast then headed out to see the supposed chicken ranch. Around 12:30 p.m., once Gruber had gotten his friend off the beaten path and into the woods, he attacked him and tried to rob him. In the frenzy, he unfortunately crushed the man's skull. (Gruber later confessed that his unsuspecting friend only had twenty dollars in his pockets.) Panicked, Gruber dragged the man's body into the bushes and covered it up. He then boarded a train at 1:15 p.m. and headed to Spokane.

Stupidly, Gruber decided to sell the deceased man's watch in Spokane at a pawn shop on the corner of Stevens and Main Streets.

Billings's body was later found off Fifteenth Street in Coeur d'Alene by two horrified teenagers, Charles Seagraves and Luther Mashburne. It was still partially covered by some branches. In the dead man's pocket was a crumpled and well-worn letter from his daughter, Emma Wyer; another letter from his sister and a third from a friend. No money was found on his person, since Gruber had stolen it. His body was stiff and was carted off to the Coeur d'Alene Morgue.

Coroner Wenz determined that Billings had been murdered early on that tragic day, sometime before noon. He suffered four deep gashes to his head and a fractured skull. He had been seriously beaten, too.

The police were ready to search for his brutal killer, and they were pretty sure they knew who he was, but they had a hard time locating Gruber. Eventually, months later, the police finally located Gruber. He was being held in jail in Lewiston for bootlegging. Sheriff Bailey charged him for Billings's murder, and he was sent back to Coeur d'Alene for his trial. While Gruber pleaded not guilty, he was convicted of murder in the first degree.

Weeks later, just two hours away from swinging from the noose, Gruber was miraculously pardoned. He received a commutation of his sentence that lowered his punishment to life in prison. He had argued that he "never had a chance at life." And once the boy's horrific past came to life, it was hard to not feel sorry for him.

But he was still a coldblooded killer.

Gruber's story begins with his birth in Texas. His early childhood was one of a personal tragedy—so horrible that it is close to unimaginable. At a young age, he was the sole eyewitness to his father's brutal murder of his mother with an axe, and then his father committed suicide as well. The traumatized boy was shuffled to several orphanages in Iowa; he endured this until he turned sixteen. Then he ran away. And although he was free, he was both broke and homeless. With no real direction in life, he joined the Parker Carnival Company. And that is where he became friends with John Billings.

On January 18, 1910, the *Coeur d'Alene Evening News* wrote up the story of Gruber's confession. Gruber stated, "I suppose I will hang for this, but I don't care." The officers then told him, "We know you hit Billings harder than you intended to, now didn't you?" Gruber hung his head and said,

Fred Gruber's mock hangman's noose dangled above his jail cell's ceiling. Gruber asked the guards, "How does that look, boys? Great thing, eh?" *Courtesy of David of Washington, D.C., Wikimedia Commons,* Hangman Rope Displayed at the National Museum of Crime and Punishment, Washington, D.C.

"Yes, I did not intend to hit him as hard as I did, but when I saw what was done, I then had to finish the deal."

After his appeal, Gruber only pleaded guilty to the robbery, but the judge determined he wasn't going to let him off so easily. During his trial, Gruber always remained strangely calm and indifferent. He never showed signs of remorse for the death of his friend.

A man named Fred Andrews came and visited him once when he was at the sheriff's office. When they saw one another, Andrews oddly said, "Hello, Carlisle, how are you? Well, you sure are a pretty bird, aren't you?" Then they began chatting about bootlegging in Lewiston.

Throughout the trial, Gruber was laughing and in good spirits. He appeared to have no fear about being sentenced to death. When he received a county shave at the barbershop, Gruber laughed and told the officer, "Nothing is too good for me, and I want all that is going."

The pawn broker William Goldbott testified against Gruber, showing receipt no. 7958, dated December 4, for $7.50, the value of Billings's watch, signed by Gruber himself. After several more months of trials and appeals, Judge Dunn had had enough of the boy's nonsense. The judge looked at Gruber and said, "You shall be hung by the neck until you are dead on Friday, May 20."

Gruber had received the death sentence a second time. The judge then looked at the teenager and continued, "You are soon to be ushered to a higher court, and I advise you to prepare for it....You are a young man and are soon to meet death. Think well of the matter and arrange your plans accordingly."

Back at the sheriff's office, Gruber calmly lit a cigarette and said, "The judge was a little shaky, wasn't he?"

In his cell, Gruber toyed with a piece of rope. He made a mock noose and hung it from the ceiling above his cot. He told the guard, "How does that look, boys? Great thing, eh?"

Before his hanging, Gruber remained calm, slept well and had a good appetite.

The townspeople must have wondered as they read the news and followed the trial how hardened was Gruber that he killed his only friend, robbed him of a pittance and then pawned his watch—only to land himself swinging from the rope until he was pronounced dead?

Perhaps some people are just wicked to the bone.

The Franklin Hotel Fire: Accident or Arson?

The Franklin Hotel fire on September 16, 1908, was shrouded in mystery. How did it start? Was it started on purpose? The Franklin fire that destroyed the entire building and killed two men still remains unsolved.

The wickedness and devastation caused from arson is overwhelming. With a mere flick of a match, an entire city can be reduced to ashes, its citizens often left with nothing, as most did not carry insurance.

The Franklin Block fire was the third that Coeur d'Alene had suffered in just two months; the Fraternal Hall was completely destroyed by fire, as was the town auditorium that July. The auditorium fire was also thought to be caused by arson. It is no wonder that so many residents feared there was an arsonist or two roaming their town.

When locals smelled the obvious odor of smoke, they knew the city could be completely destroyed. In an era when fire equipment and services were minimal, a fire could destroy a city within hours.

Luckily for downtown Coeur d'Alene, this fire was somewhat controlled. The Coeur d'Alene Bank and Trust was destroyed and the nearby Hotel Idaho suffered damage, but the destruction could have been a lot worse.

The two men who lost their lives in the flames were Gus Layton and Jacob Skogland.

So, was the tragic fire a true accident or intentional chaos created by an arsonist?

Frank Deegan, a friend of Skogland, was the bartender at the Franklin Hotel and also the person who first discovered the fire. He smelled smoke and saw the flickering of flames peeking through the dumbwaiter. Deegan also noticed that he smelled the faint odor of either kerosene or gas. He quickly sounded the fire alarm.

After talking to witnesses and employees of the hotel, the police considered several suspects and interviewed multiple witnesses.

Suspect 1: Mike Shomer stated that at 8:00 p.m., he was in his room, where he remained until the time of the fire alarm. In reality, Shomer was drinking at the Lakeview Bar, then he ran to the hotel when he heard of the fire to gather his belongings. He lied, which is why he became a prime suspect. Why did he have to lie? What was he hiding?

Suspect 2: Another suspect (who was later charged with perjury) was Joseph Joyce, who said he had come to Coeur d'Alene from Spokane for "some fun." He claimed he was back in his room around 10:30 p.m. and sleeping at the time of the fire. His room was next to the kitchen area, and he said he also smelled gas and that he thought the fire was started in the kitchen. Joyce maintained that he ran out of the hotel, fearing for his life, but then he wanted to return to his room to grab the twenty-eight dollars he had left on his nightstand. After interviewing some workers on the docks, the police discovered Joyce was lying and that he was actually loitering around the wharf during the time of the fire. Police later apprehended him, and the jury found him guilty. When they searched him in jail, they found that he had over twenty skeleton keys in his possession. What were all the keys for? What doors did they open? Why did he lie about his whereabouts during the fire if he had nothing to hide?

Suspect 3: Mrs. Kidd came out from the kitchen area, acting anxiously and concealing something in her arms under a cloth. Witnesses told police that she was acting very strangely. Was she holding the kerosene that was used to ignite the fire? Her story changed each time she was interviewed by the police.

There were also several witnesses to the fire.

Witness 1: One witness to the fire was Mr. William Gurly (Gourly) a resident of Coeur d'Alene who was drinking that evening at the Franklin Hotel. He insisted that, earlier that night, he helped a man named Horrigan up to the same room where Gus Layton was.

On his way back down to the bar, he saw Mrs. Kidd (suspect 3) coming out from one of the rooms downstairs, holding a strange object covered with a cloth. She seemed extremely startled when she saw Gurly and moved back into the room from which she came. What was she carrying? Was it really a container of kerosene? Did she start the fire? What would her motive have been? Gurly told the woman that Horrigan would want the room for a few more weeks. She seemed not to care.

Witness 2: Around the same time, Deegan (the bartender at Franklin) was walking up the stairs, and Gurly followed behind him. As they reached the top of the stairs, the smoke was so thick that the men were forced to go back. They both quickly moved outside to the safety of the street to get some fresh air. As they coughed and caught their breath, they soon heard hollering coming from above. It was Mr. Horrigan frantically hanging his head out the window and screaming. Thinking quickly, Gurly and Deegan grabbed a nearby ladder to help Horrigan come down to safety. Horrigan later said that Layton had also come to the window to escape the flames but that an unknown person called for him to come back. Why would Layton return to the fire when he could have gotten to safety by escaping through the window? Who called for him and why? Layton's decision to return ultimately cost him his life. His body was found burned to a crisp the next morning, along with Skogland's.

Suspect 3's version: Under oath, Mrs. Kidd told her story. She claimed that she was in bed when she heard the fire alarm and that she ran out of her room half naked and immediately ran to the safety of the street. If this was true, why did Gurly see her downstairs in another room during the fire? And if she was half naked, wouldn't Gurly have remembered that? She also said nothing of meeting Gurly or disclosed the item that she was carrying in her arms. Her story didn't fit, and she was clearly lying on the witness stand as well. Why? What was her motive?

Witness 3: Thomas Deegan (the brother of Frank, the bartender) was also a witness. He claimed he had retired to bed around 11:30 p.m. but did not fall asleep right away. During that time, he heard someone come up the stairs, move past his door, go down the hallway and then, after a few moments, return the same way had come. It was five minutes later that the fire alarm was sounded. He could also smell the faint odor of gasoline.

When the firefighters arrived, they quickly assessed that the Franklin Hotel was beyond rescue and turned their efforts to saving the neighboring buildings. The fire had spread to the Wright and Steele building that was occupied by the hardware store. The flames engulfed the Coeur d'Alene Bank and Trust and threatened the Hotel Idaho as well. The firemen worked tirelessly to quench the flames.

The county and the owners of the building, Young and McBurney, offered a $500 reward for the capture of the arsonist. Chief McGovern was sure he could find them.

On September 22, McGovern's wish came true. Through his persistence and great detective work, he proved that Joyce truly had been lying. Two night watchmen, Ernest Miner and Calvin Gardner, came forward and told McGovern that Joyce had been sleeping on one of the boats of the Red Collar line the night of the fire.

Was Joyce the arsonist? He finally confessed to lying about his whereabouts at the start of the Franklin fire disaster during the inquest held by Coroner T.E. Hadel, and he was promptly sent to the jail in Rathdrum. No other articles can be found to determine whether Joyce was the actual arsonist or if he just lied about where he was at the time of the fire.

So many livelihoods were destroyed by the fire that started that night. During the time of the fire, the hotel portion was located on the upper level (its proprietors were Mr. and Mrs. Joe Johnson, who were away at the time), and various stores were occupying the lower level.

Some of the lives and businesses ruined (not all had insurance or were grossly under-covered) were:

- Peter Bergleen, the proprietor of the saloon.
- A cigar and confection shop on the west end of the building.
- Oscar Foster Men's Clothing Store.
- Mother's Kitchen, run by G.E. Curry.
- Mrs. O'Brien and her dressmaking shop.
- A German bakery run by Schuttle and Kelvey.
- A restaurant run by Atwood Manthei.

The business losses aside, two innocent men lost their lives in a horrifying way; they were burned alive. Not much is known about Gus Layton except he was approximately thirty years old and had been checked into room 11 that fateful night. Jacob Skogland was only twenty-eight years old and was residing in room 14 at the Franklin Hotel. He had come to Coeur d'Alene in search of employment. He had become friends with the bartender, Deegan, and the two were actually planning on going out boating the very next day. Skogland was born on September 5, 1880, in Norway to his parents, John and Mathilda Skogland. He was buried at the Ely Cemetery in Minnesota.

The Magruder Robbers: Captured by a Premonition

Nothing could be more horrendous than the gruesome, pathetic and brutal killing of the innocent and hardworking Lloyd Magruder Jr. (1825–1863).

Magruder came to his grisly end one dark night in the summer of 1863 at the hands of a group of trusted men who were traveling with him and his train of mules, which were carrying supplies and a large amount of gold dust. The murder was considered one of north Idaho's most wicked crimes and one that lingered in the locals' minds long after they finished reading about it. The incident eventually led to the first legal hangings in the Idaho Territory.

The story begins in the 1860s, when Magruder began packing and selling mining supplies over the mountains. He was a well-respected, prominent citizen. He was also one of the state's oldest pioneers, as Magruder had come to work in Idaho around 1862. He was one of the very first to blaze a trail into the untamed Canyon Creek area. He was one of the leaders in the discovery of the profitable John Day Mine. Magruder also owned a profitable grocery store. They say it was at his very own store that

Pack trains such as this one, seen running through the Coeur d'Alene National Forest, were common, and some trains had over sixty mules and horses to control. *Courtesy of the Boston Public Library, from the Tichnor Brothers Collection.*

Magruder met the murderous men who later traveled with him and sealed his tragic fate.

In 1863, Magruder moved on from Lewiston to the Bannock Mines in Montana with fifty mules, eight horses and a good load of supplies. The Bannock Mines were almost empty, as most men had moved on to a new discovery at Grasshopper Creek. Magruder sold his wares at a makeshift shop, traded some mules and sold the supplies anyway, which earned him a very hefty chunk of change. Stories vary, but it is said that he managed to sell about $10,000 worth of goods and mules and was then the proud owner of approximately ninety-four pounds of gold dust. (Gold dust was the only form of legal tender back then, as greenbacks were discounted and frowned upon when used. This amount of gold dust would be worth almost $2 million today.)

The men packed up and left Bannock to make their way back to Lewiston. The trip back home was three hundred long and winding miles on horseback.

Three men caught wind of Magruder's wealth and began to devise a plot to rob him. These three men were Daniel "Doc" Howard, George Christopher Lower (Lowery) and James Romaine. They took another worker named Page aside and whispered to him their plan to rob and kill Magruder. But Page was no killer and wanted no part in their plan.

On October 3, the men set out to head back to Lewiston. On this particular trip, Magruder had no reason not to trust the group of men who accompanied him: William Phillips, Charles Allen, Daniel "Doc" Howard, George Christopher Lowery, James Romaine, William Page and two brothers named Horace and Robert Chalmers. Magruder hired the group to help handle and care for the mule train and for protection on the long journey. The men all seemed to get along, and they became friends. Some of the men offered much-needed services for the trip; Lowery was a trained blacksmith, "Doc" had good knowledge of medicine and Page was a trapper and guide who knew his way through the mountains.

After a few days of travel, on the evening of October 8, the men decided to stop for the night and set up camp. Magruder and Lowery were scheduled to be on duty for the first watch. The rest of the men claimed to be tired and went to bed. After some time by the fire, Magruder and Lowery heard the mules stomping around, so they decided to go check on them and make sure they had water. The men moved away from the fire and into the darkness of the woods. Magruder noticed that as they walked toward the mules, Lowery grabbed a nearby axe. Magruder paused for a minute and wondered why Lowery would need an axe. When asked, Lowery claimed he was going to build a fence to make sure the mules stayed put for the night. Magruder thought this was very strange, and if he had followed his intuition then, he might have survived. Instead, the men slowly walked over to the mules.

That was the last time Magruder took a breath or looked into the starry night.

Lowery quickly brought the axe down onto Magruder's skull, crushing it.

Around midnight, Page heard Renton and Lowery outside and saw that the men, then carrying axes, went into a nearby tent. Next, moans and loud cries could be heard coming from the two brothers, Horace and Robert Chalmers. Blood spatter was thrown across the canvas tent as they were hacked to pieces. Then there was only silence—but not for long. Renton quickly grabbed his gun and shot the stunned and terrified Charles Allen, killing him instantly. Nearby, William Phillips stood frozen in fear and scared for his life, as he had just witnessed the men killing the others in cold blood.

Without hesitation, Romaine moved toward Phillips with the axe, yelling, "You fool! I told you at Virginia City not to come. You had no business to come. I wish Jim Rhodes had come instead, for I have wanted to kill him for a long time!" Then he proceeded to kill Phillips with the axe.

William Page stood, completely paralyzed, knowing he would be the next victim in the bloody massacre. As the men looked into each other's eyes, a silent meeting of the minds took place. Surprisingly, the killers calmly told the terrified Page to go look after the mules. Page was apparently spared his life because he knew the routes like the back of his hand and could help them get back to town.

The murderers had to devise a plan to dispose of the evidence and the bodies.

They decided to roll the bodies up in a canvas tent and roll them down a nearby hill and into a ravine. Magruder's bloody body was still where Lowery had left it. The rest of the bags, gear and evidence were thrown into the fire to burn. After the evidence was burned, they gathered up any remaining iron, put it in a bag and buried it under a big log.

For some unknown reason (possibly because it would be highly suspicious if the men were seen traveling with Magruder's large team of mules without him), the killers decided to make the night even more horrific. They shot almost all of the eighty mules but kept the eight horses. They had also brought moccasins with them, premeditating that if they wore the moccasins, whoever stumbled across the crime scene would tend to believe that the murders had been committed by Natives and not White men.

Once the gruesome task of tossing the bodies and burning evidence was done, they divvied up Magruder's gold, mounted their horses and headed back toward Lewiston. The terrified Page was leading the way back to town. There are no records about whether Page got any of the gold dust. Along the way, the men found a local rancher to take care of the extra horses and tack for them until spring, paying the rancher with Magruder's hard-earned money.

How the killers slept that night at the Hotel de France in Lewiston is a mystery. But the next morning, on October 19, they loaded their belongings up in a stagecoach and were soon heading off toward Walla Walla, Washington.

But they did not plan on one very strange thing that would eventually bring them to justice.

The very same night they brutally murdered Lloyd Magruder, Magruder's best friend, Hilary "Hill" Beachy (1822–1875), had a gut-wrenching premonition in the form of a nightmare about the murder. In his dream, he had the sickening image of his friend with his face and neck bloody, killed by an axe.

When Beachy woke in a start, he somehow knew his friend was dead. He didn't know how he knew it, but he did. Did his best friend really come to him in a dream to let him know of his terrible fate? Was it possible? Throughout the day, Beachy could not shrug off the dream, no matter how hard he tried. He began asking around to see if anyone had seen Magruder lately—no one had.

Then, when another packer came riding into Lewiston, a man who had left after Magruder, Beachy knew in his heart that Magruder had met trouble, as his friend should have arrived long before the other man did.

Interestingly (and here is where coincidence comes into play), when the murderers inquired about four tickets for a stagecoach that headed from Lewiston to Walla Walla, they did so at Beachy's own stagecoach line. And Beachy had another stroke of odd luck; he actually remembered one of the men's faces—from his dream.

But Beachy remained cool and calm behind his desk. He did not want to tip the men off and scare them away before he could hopefully secure more information about them. He told the men that the office was closed but that he would take their names down on the waybill for the morning's trip. They gave him the fake names of John and Joseph Smith and Tom and Jim Jones. Beachy became even more suspicious, as he knew they were lying.

As the men were checking into their rooms at the Hotel de France in town and getting ready to sleep off the long trip, Beachy decided he had to snoop around and find out more about these men. He asked his good friend Judge John G. Berry to help him out.

The two men soon discovered that the suspects had boarded their horses at a nearby ranch. Beachy and Berry quickly set out toward the ranch. Upon their arrival, Beachy began looking over the horses the men had left there, and he suddenly recognized Magruder's personal saddle in the barn. His heart sank. He was pretty sure Magruder did not sell his favorite saddle to one of these rough-looking men. Why in the world would he need to sell his favorite saddle when he had plenty of money?

Beachy was more certain than ever that the men had killed his friend and immediately began begging the judge for an arrest warrant on these four killers. But even as he somehow miraculously managed to secure a warrant, reality began to come into play. What was Beachy thinking—all of this speculation on just a dream, a hunch and an abandoned saddle? It seemed ridiculous, but Beachy somehow knew he was on the right path. His mind was made up, and he was going to follow these men to Walla Walla and have them apprehended by local authorities.

As his wife fretted about his rash decision to leave unexpectedly, Beachy began preparing for his trip.

There are several valid reasons why Beachy should absolutely not have left Lewiston on a hunch:

1. He really could not afford to leave his two businesses—the Luna House and his stagecoach line.
2. He was not a policeman or lawman.
3. He knew nothing about the killers, not even their real names, as they checked in under false identities.
4. He didn't know if Magruder was dead or alive.
5. He was also putting his own life in harm's way if these men really were coldblooded killers.

But Beachy could not be persuaded to remain in Lewiston and do nothing except pray Magruder would eventually return, safe and sound.

The next morning, as the killers got inside the stagecoach to head on their way, Beachy and Berry poked their heads into the wagon and demanded the men to show them their tickets. As they complied, Beachy and Berry both took a good, hard look at the men's faces, burning them into their memories for future reference.

As the coach began to prepare for its departure, Beachy suddenly felt panic set in and quickly turned to his friend and said, "Please judge, Lloyd Magruder has been murdered, and the four men on that stage are his

Stagecoaches like this one from 1869 were easy targets for villains, and drivers were putting their lives on the line every trip. The individuals pictured are unidentified. *Courtesy of Wikimedia Commons, public domain, U.S. National Archives.*

murderers! Will you swear me in as a deputy and go with the sheriff and me to arrest them?" Although the judge agreed, something did not sit right; he was still confused. What tangible proof did they have? He reminded Beachy that Magruder's wife, Margaret, had just received a letter from him saying he would be back home in Lewiston in about twelve days. It was possible that Magruder's saddle was simply stolen, his plans delayed or he was experiencing trouble with his pack of mules.

But Beachy could not shake the dreaded feeling that his friend had been murdered, no matter what the judge said to reassure him. In town, rumors began to circulate, and some folks thought that perhaps Beachy was losing his mind—it was only a dream. There was no real evidence that these men had killed Magruder.

So, against Beachy's intuition, the carriage left in a trail of dust, leaving Beachy to figure out his next move. The coach would soon have

a few hours' head start—valuable time lost when tracking killers. After a quick prayer for guidance, Beachy kissed his wife goodbye, packed a bag and climbed aboard a stagecoach himself to travel the ninety long miles to Walla Walla. Upon his arrival there, he found the men had already boarded a steamer that was heading to Portland, Oregon, via the Columbia River. Unwilling to give up his pursuit, he also slowly made his way to Portland. When he finally arrived in Oregon, much to Beachy's dismay, the men had already jumped another steamer that was heading to San Francisco, California. As luck would have it, no other steamers were leaving Portland for San Francisco for another ten days.

It seemed the odds were against Beachy after all his hard work, time and travel. He would have to be patient and think of a new plan. He did not have ten days to waste. He quickly boarded another stagecoach that was heading to Yreka, California, because, at the time, it was the only place one could secure telegraph services to San Francisco.

Once in Yreka, he quickly telegraphed the police chief in San Francisco, Martin Burke, explained the situation and demanded that he apprehend

Lloyd Magruder's killers left town in a stagecoach heading to San Francisco. Their plans were ruined by Magruder's best friend, Beachy, who later arrested them. *Courtesy of Fishel & Co., Deadwood, South Dakota, the Library of Congress.*

the men and hold them. Burke assigned the unusual case to detective Isaiah Lees, and it was decided that the criminals would be captured and detained as they came off the boat.

When the unsuspecting men debarked, they were apprehended by the local authorities as planned. Beachy could relax for now. But the justice system was as fallible then as it is now, and the killers were able to hire a fancy lawyer named Alexander Campbell (since they had a bunch of Magruder's gold dust to pay for it), who filed a suit for writ of habeas corpus, which basically demands the authorities to "show the body," or they could not detain the men. Of course, there were no bodies to show. The men's lawyer also claimed that the governor had no right to issue the warrant and outlined other legal technicalities and improper procedures.

Beachy refused to back down and demanded permission to extradite the man back to Idaho for a trial. After his long travels to capture these men, he would not just allow them to go free. Eventually, Beachy was granted the required permission to take the prisoners back to Idaho.

Upon arriving in Lewiston, the killers encountered a large and angry crowd that had gathered to wait for them. For the safety of the prisoners and the locals, the criminals were kept upstairs, guarded (and heavily ironed with shackles) in Beachy's hotel, the Luna House. Page was kept away from the other men, alone in another room. A reporter tried to take a photograph of the men, but Lowery decided to destroy the camera. When asked why he did this, he oddly replied, "I thought it was loaded!" Lowery had obviously never seen a camera before and thought it was some sort of gun.

Page swore under oath that he took no part in the robbing and killing of Magruder or his mules and offered to turn over actual evidence to help convict the assassins. He did state that he helped burn evidence, but he participated due to sheer fear. He had just witnessed the entire clan be bludgeoned to death. His testimony was crucial for the trial, as it secured that the three men had opportunity and motive for the killings—as well as the fact that Page actually witnessed the killings. Page led authorities back to the scene of the crime, where the bodies were still wrapped in the canvas tents in the ravine. The buried brass and iron fittings were not found.

After the trial, on the evening of January 23, 1864, the three men were found guilty and were scheduled to hang until their deaths on March 4. The scaffold was erected in town at Judge Poe's house, and the three killers were walked to their terrible (but well deserved) fate of hanging from the gallows until their necks broke. As the noose was tightened around Lowery's neck, he bizarrely said, "Launch your old boat; it's nothing but an old mud scow anyway!" (He had also left an obscene letter in his room to be read later.)

The *Evening Bulletin* in San Francisco stated, "In the whole record of crime, three murders more coldblooded, instigated only by a lust for the hard-earned gold of others, can scarcely be found."

If Beachy had not acted on his dream, even though many were making fun of him, would the murderers of his best friend have ever been captured? Probably not. Beachy was a great man to follow through with his hunch and bring punishment to these horrible and greedy, good-for-nothing men.

Interesting facts:

- Beachy received $6,240 as reimbursement him for his hard work and troubles.
- Page was later shot and killed by a man named Albert Igo while visiting a house of prostitution for unknown reasons.

Left: Llyod Magruder. *Courtesy of Liz O'Hara.*

Right: The three killers of Lloyd Magruder were sentenced to hang on January 23, 1864, at a scaffold like this one that was erected in front of Judge Poe's house. *Courtesy of Pearson Scott Foresman, public domain, Wikimedia Commons.*

- Of the $25,000 stolen from Magruder, the remaining $17,000 that was confiscated from the killers was given to Caroline Magruder.
- These hangings would be recorded as the first legal hangings in the Idaho Territory.
- Beachy died of a stroke in San Francisco in 1875.
- In 1992, two men named Monty Spears and Tom Haugstad visited the murder site along the Nez Perce Trail with metal detectors. They were able to locate rusty harness buckles, nails and .33-caliber lead shot under a few inches of dirt, approximately where the bag of burned items was hidden. (Read the full article here: www.deseret.com.)

Note: In 1980, the U.S. Forest Service named and now maintains a 101-mile-long road (Forest Road 468), the Magruder Corridor, that runs through Idaho and Montana. This is the trail Magruder used on his fateful trip. At approximately mile marker 44.2 westbound (near the Selway River), you pass the site where Magruder's body was found.

Fence Line Dispute Turns Into a Bloodbath

On March 25, 1910, as the clock tower chimed 11:00 a.m., the sound of a pistol shot rang through Second and Sherman Streets in Coeur d'Alene. A man quickly fell onto the sidewalk in front of the Lake City Hardware Company Store in the Graham Block on Third Street and Sherman Avenue, bleeding. Soon, dozens of people crowded the street to see what was going on, unintentionally destroying any possible evidence.

Before the fatal shooting on Sherman Avenue, Crone had gone to Hudlow's house, carrying a large rock, which he intended to hit Hudlow on the head with. After a brief amount of cussing and threatening between the two men, the red-faced Crone finally yelled, "Very well, I'll see you later and give you plenty!"

The day of the shooting started out innocently enough; Hudlow and a friend named Will Rickley were down by the water, working on his boat, *Totem*, fixing the boiler. They soon discovered that the boiler needed a few more parts, so they went into town and headed up to the Lake City Hardware Store to buy them. They saw grumpy Crone standing in front of the Office Saloon near the hardware store with another man. Crone saw Hudlow and started muttering angry threats at him. Hudlow said, "Go back! I don't want any trouble!" But Crone continued to head toward Hudlow. Hudlow, thinking Crone was going to attack him, quickly drew his gun and fired.

Witnesses Judge A.V. Chamberlain and S.A. Varnam were busy talking on the sidewalk when they saw two men walking toward them. They stated that, unexpectantly, one of the men, Russell Hudlow, pulled a revolver from his jacket and fired the gun at the other man, George Crone. Crone fell to the ground instantly. Hudlow, seemingly unsatisfied with his results, raised his arm to fire at Crone a second time. Chamberlain acted quickly and was able to grab the man's arm before another shot rang through Crone's wounded body. Another witness, Sheriff Adams, was standing across the street when the commotion occurred. He pounced on Hudlow and extracted the .38-caliber Smith & Wesson revolver from his hand.

The bleeding Crone soon became confused and delirious. The men helped him move into the safety of the hardware store. When they inspected him, they realized Crone had been shot under his heart and that the bullet had traveled through his left lung and out the back of his body. Crone was taken to the hospital for treatment; there, the doctors realized that the bullet had caused both of his legs to be paralyzed, as his spinal cord had been seriously injured.

The stunned spectators on the street were bewildered, wondering what on earth could have caused such a scene.

It was a simple fence dispute.

The two men had been arguing over a fence boundary for some time. The men lived next to each other on Hayden Lake. Their farms were two miles apart, but that was not enough distance to satisfy the men. Crone was certain that Hudlow's fence was on his property, so he tore down the fence in anger. Crone had even gone so far as to shoot Hudlow's dog.

At the trial, Hudlow contested that the shooting was in self-defense as Crone had been constantly threatening his life. Judge Probate Egbers charged Hudlow with assault with intent to commit murder, and bail was set for a whopping $10,000. Crone remained in stable condition and was said to be permanently paralyzed by the bullet wound.

SUICIDE OR MURDER?

The tragic story of a young man, aged twenty-seven at the time of his mysterious death, remains unsolved to this day. The details of his untimely demise are nothing more than a few written sketchy paragraphs with conflicting clues and facts in the newspapers. Even his burial and final resting place remain a secret.

His life was taken on a cold afternoon in late August 1906.

Night watchman Cark Kronblandt was making his usual rounds on the streets of downtown Coeur d'Alene when he suddenly heard gunshots. There were a total of five shots fired in rapid succession. He quickly ran from his location in front of the Office Saloon and made his way toward the direction of the shooting. When he arrived, the dying teenager was lying on the ground near the Novelty Works building at 112 South Fifth Street and Sherman Avenue, blood pooling around what was once his head.

The officer quickly blew his whistle, calling for help. Upon his inspection of the victim, the officer noticed the revolver was still grasped tightly in his hand. One newspaper story says the gun was a .38-caliber revolver; another says it was a .45-caliber six-shooter Colt double-action. Which was it?

One thing was certain: a bullet had gone through the right side of the boy's head, killing him instantly.

Soon, Doctor Dwyer and Doctor Carik arrived, eager to save the boy, and although he was still breathing, they both determined he was beyond rescue and sure to die soon.

When the men inspected his body for any identification or clues, they did not find anything of value that could help them. They found in his pockets two beer chips, a broken pocketknife, a safety pin and two handkerchiefs. His empty holster, attached to a U.S. Army belt, looked brand-new and had the letters "J.W." stamped in the leather. The man's hands were not that of a laborer, as they were soft and uncalloused. His clothes were cheaply made. He wore a sort of tennis shoe. On his bloody hand were two rings, those that maybe a druggist might wear. His skin made the men believe that he was possibly a foreigner.

The watchman revealed that right after the shooting, he noticed a small carriage with a single horse quickly moving away from the crime scene. There were three men sitting in the buggy. The driver was lashing his poor horse, trying to get it to run faster. The carriage moved behind the fireman's hose cart house, crossed the electric railway tracks and made its way through the Coeur d'Alene Lumber Company's yard.

The boy was rushed to the hospital to be treated, but it looked grim. The last of the five bullets had become lodged in his brain. The mystery man was still somewhat conscious, and everyone hoped that he would wake up long enough to at least name his killer or state why he had shot himself.

Meanwhile, attorney Whitla returned to the bloody scene and found four more bullets littered where the unknown man had fallen. After questioning locals and shopkeepers, he found that no one had seen anything suspicious.

Unfortunately, the wounded man did not retain consciousness and soon died from the gunshot wound to his head. His body was taken to Idaho Undertaking in town.

There were so many unanswered questions. Who was this man? Why did he get shot? Who were the three men in the buggy, and were they actually guilty of murder or simply getting away from the mayhem out of fear for their own lives? Was the victim an army deserter, or was he suffering from depression? Did the deceased shoot at his killer (or killers) first and then the fifth shot the watchman heard was the one that killed him?

One ridiculous suggestion offered was that the man shot himself in the head and then the muscles in his hand fired off the other four shots due to a reflex. That is highly unlikely.

The Kyriss Mystery

On May 9, 1908, the body of a man was found floating in the Coeur d'Alene River near downtown. The victim had suffered extensive wounds. Coroner Wenz recorded that a trauma to the head, caused by an unknown object, punctured his forehead; the object penetrated the brain, which caused hemorrhaging. He had been dead between seven and ten days before being discovered. The victim was Christopher Kyriss.

Joe Johnson, the proprietor of the Franklin Hotel in Coeur d'Alene, was Kyriss's friend for over seven years. He stated that Kyriss had rented a room at his hotel, and when he was checking in, he appeared very nervous. He arrived alone and was never seen with anyone else. When he ran into Kyriss the next morning, he still seemed upset, and when asked if he was going to go eat breakfast, Kyriss oddly replied, "Going to get a morning's morning, then go to breakfast." Johnson had no inclination that that morning would be the last time he ever saw his friend Kyriss alive.

Another friend, John Munch of Spokane, had been Kyriss's friend even longer—about nineteen years. He said he had last seen Kyriss on April 26. Although Kyriss had over $400 in the bank and would, at times, drink heavily and spend money freely, he was known to actually carry very little cash on his person.

His wife told reporters that the last time she saw her husband was on April 7. He told her he was going downtown to the meat market and that he would return soon. She noticed that he took with him two bank books, a six-shooter and a change of shoes—strange items to take to the meat market.

At the meat market, it was discovered that Kyriss had ordered some meat and then did not have the two dollars on him to pay, so he told the butcher he was going to go to the bank to get the money. He never returned for his two-dollar meat purchase.

After Kyriss's body was discovered, both the Coeur d'Alene and Spokane police decided to work together on the case. They discovered that Kyriss had gone to Spokane on April 28 to pawn his gold watch. The pawn dealer told the police that Kyriss often pawned his watch for quick cash but always came back and retrieved it. It was a beautifully engraved watch with a heavy gold chain. They also learned that Kyriss had told a friend that he was going to travel to Ritzville to collect $800 that was owed to him. Who was the person who owed Kyriss such a large sum?

Coroner Wenz's autopsy reported that Kyriss's forehead had been penetrated by a circular object and that his lungs did not contain any water, so he was killed prior to being tossed in the river. He also had a missing index finger on his left hand. Munch told police that the finger was missing a while ago and that that is what helped him identify the body of his friend. Was this the motive—robbery and murder? Had he retrieved the $800 from the unknown person, only to have that person attack and kill him later? (Kyriss did not have the $800 in cash on his body when he was found.)

The police felt Kyriss had been tricked into drinking with someone then lured to the area of Tubb's Hill, where he was assaulted, robbed and his body thrown into the lake.

Munch, very worried about what happened to Kyriss, went to the scene of the crime and found Kyriss's hat and coat placed neatly on a tree stump near where his body was found. He thought this was odd. Did Kyriss or his assailant neatly place his coat and hat on the stump? Why?

A $500 reward was offered by the county for information leading to the arrest of Kyriss's murderer. No one was ever arrested or convicted for the crime. The horrible murder of Christopher Kyriss remains unsolved to this day.

4
ROBBERS, GAMBLING AND SWINDLING

The fantastic city of Coeur d'Alene was not immune from crime, unfortunately. The incredible beauty of the area did not magically repel criminals and thieves. There are many records reporting all types of crimes committed for a multitude of reasons by all kinds of people. In Coeur d'Alene's early years, women were committing as many crimes as men. Many offenses were caused by nothing more than greed, while others truly were mere accidents. Other crimes were just odd, at best.

A humorous reported crime that received a seemingly excessive penalty was that of a man named Oscar Snyder. He was sentenced to jail for up to fourteen years—for stealing some chickens.

In 1908, Mike Banas and Joe Huser were charged with robbery when they stole ten pennies and a worthless, unredeemable New Brunswick bill from the money drawer of A. Pierce, who owned the Cigar & Confectionery Store on Sherman Street. Ten cents hardly seem worth the trouble of breaking and entering, let alone jail time.

Some other peculiar Coeur d'Alene crimes that are listed in the *Inmates of Idaho Penitentiary, 1864–1974* collection are:

- In 1885, the youngest inmate, ten-year-old James Baker, was committed for shooting a man to death in the Soda Springs Saloon, where his dad worked.
- In 1896, John Burns was arrested for stealing two dollars from his sleeping friend to buy another round of drinks at

John Banks Saloon, costing him several months behind bars and added a grand larceny charge to his record.
- In 1923, a seventeen-year-old boy named Lester Thompson was recorded as a criminal type because his "ears were small and close to his head."
- In 1940, a man named Melvin Yeager served time for forging a ten-dollar check to buy his sweet wife a new washing machine—now that's love.

Compared to crimes committed on a daily basis today, it is humorous (and sad) what people were charged with back in the old days. In some states back then, stealing horses or livestock would find the criminal at the end of a noose.

Many crimes were committed in the Coeur d'Alene region because of the silver, gold, lead and zinc that was discovered in the mines as early as the 1880s. The Silver Valley is cradled between the Coeur d'Alene Mountains and the Bitterroot Range in northern Idaho. The area has produced more silver than any other region in Idaho. Mining claims were often "jumped," which would cause great fury. Claim jumping meant that a person illegally took possession of a claim that had previously been staked by another individual, and it was very common. This led to the rule that a claim had to actually be worked to keep it, thus cutting down on the number of claims people owned but never took the time to actually work. It would be hard to pin down how many murders, shootings and deaths were caused by mining claims.

Pickpockets and petty thieves were big irritations to local police in Coeur d'Alene. Pickpockets were almost impossible to catch, as they were as quick as magicians and could rob a person without the victim noticing anything but the slightest bump against them. Often working in pairs, the pickpocket duo would find their "mark" (victim) and then make their move. The person in charge of stealing was termed the "tool," and the person in charge of distracting the mark was called the "stall." Usually, the pickpockets loitered near a bank, so when the unsuspecting person left the institution with money in their wallet, their chances of stealing a greater amount of money increased.

In Coeur d'Alene, the pickpockets would hover near the depot, and they would expertly rob people before they boarded the train to Spokane. Some of the notorious Coeur d'Alene pick pockets were J. Wilson, Mike Lynch and R.H. Keller. These guys would casually steal anything they could easily get away with, like watches, jewelry, bills, coins—even cameras. The petty crime got so bad that local police made flyers that they posted around the depot; they read in big, bold letters: "**BEWARE OF PICKPOCKETS!**"

It is interesting how the police captured criminals in the old days, before the modern-day luxuries of forensics, DNA, fingerprints and databases. These brave and intelligent men only had such clues as missing buttons, footprints, hearsay and, hopefully, confessions. The lawmen in those days deserve a lot more credit than they probably ever received.

Kootenai County Train Robbery

The conductor of the Northern Pacific Railway car no. 3 was surprised by two masked men late one August night in 1908. Smoothly heading through the Coeur d'Alenes en route to the west, there was no sign of trouble that night—that is, until they heard their mail car being uncoupled when they stopped at the Rathdrum Station.

In Rathdrum, two veiled men began waving around their .45-caliber pistols and a big sack of dynamite. Their threats did not go unheard, especially as soon as they started firing their guns. As the train began moving, the robbers jumped aboard. They pointed their guns at the frightened engineer, Fred Whittelsey, and yelled, "Keep it running at full speed!"

A few miles out, they ordered for the train to be stopped. There, they told the engineer and fireman to hop off and begin running for their lives. As the bullets sped past them, they did, indeed, run for their lives. Wallace Smith, the train's mail clerk, was also being shot at. A second terrified mail clerk, C.H. Raymond, was shoved back into the mail car, where the robbers stole his keys and watch then threatened to "blow his head off" if he did not show them where the money was being hidden.

Nearby, a night operator, J.W. Cahill, heard the shots and dispatched an alarm.

By the time the event was over, the robbers had fired over twenty-five shots at the men and inside the trains. When interviewing the frightened crew, it was discovered that they all felt the robbers had a good understanding of the workings of the trains. Were they possibly employees of one of the local railroads?

Frank Sturges, the fireman of car no. 3, told his side of the story: "When they got to where they told me to stand back, the tall man took hold of the

Train robberies were very common, as they carried money for the U.S. Mail. Hijacks would leave the conductors and mail clerks scared to death. *Courtesy of William Henry, photographer; Detroit Publishing Co., publisher; and the Library of Congress, item no. 2016797071.*

throttle and stopped the engine. They knew all about how to handle the engine and were perfectly familiar with every detail of handling the train."

Smith, one of the mail clerks on board, stated, "They held their guns in my face several times to compel me to reveal the rest of the money, but I told them they had all the money I knew anything about."

One of the bandits, Dan Murphy, was eventually caught and charged with the hold-up. He was identified by the engineer who had been running the train. He was found guilty by Judge Williams Huneke after a short trial and the jury deliberating for just two hours. Oddly, the prisoner was exceptionally calm and bewilderingly polite. He addressed the jury: "I just want to thank the jury for their kindness and the consideration they have gave my case, aside from the verdict."

WYATT EARP COMES TO THE COEUR D'ALENES

The name Wyatt Earp is legendary to this day. He is mostly remembered by and famous for the shoot-out at the O.K. Corral in Tombstone, Arizona. Wyatt wore many hats during his lifetime, as he was a marshal of the law, a gambler, a gunslinger, a drinker, an entrepreneur, a buffalo hunter, a saloon and brothel owner, a miner, a boxing referee and a friend to many early Hollywood stars. But he was also arrested multiple times in his life and was not always the honest man history has made him out to be. Wyatt was always chasing the almighty dollar, which tended to get him into trouble every now and then.

In 1884, when Wyatt Earp, Josie, Enright, Ferguson, Holman and Jim all traveled to the Coeur d'Alene Mountains to look at a farm for a friend and chase the local gold rush, Earp was heard saying to other fortune seekers (as he was buying six tickets for his own group), "It's the same in all gold camps. The lust for gold is overpowering—so powerful that it will lure many of these men to their deaths."

Wyatt forked over the nine dollars for the group to ride from Rathdrum to Coeur d'Alene. Once they arrived in town, they noticed how much construction was going on. They were hungry, so they stopped at the Divided Saloon on Sherman Street, where proprietor John Brown greeted them. After their meal, they inquired about heading to where the gold was supposed to be. They were told that a boat would be leaving soon and that it was launched at the north end of the river by Tony Tubb's building. The boat would travel all the way to the mission, where they would debark and head off to the Eagle City Mining Camp (near today's Murray).

The Earps didn't have much luck in the mining world, but they were smart enough to realize that the mining money could easily come to them. So, they set up a huge canvas tent and called it the White Elephant Saloon. There, they offered drinking, gambling and dancing, and it was definitely easier to make money by having the miners spend their paychecks than by prospecting. Wyatt soon became the Kootenai County deputy sheriff, which is interesting, as tales are told of the Earps hustling, not paying their taxes and jumping the mining claims of local pioneer Andrew Prichard (the latter of which could have caused him to see the end of a noose).

The Earp gang supposedly left in the dead of night, avoiding all future trouble in the Coeur d'Alene Mountains, and headed back to Texas.

Interesting Note: Another famous outlaw who came to the Coeur d'Alene Mountains was Butch Cassidy (1866–1908), whose real name was Robert LeRoy Parker, while he was being chased. It was reported that he hid a sack of gold coins while being hunted by a posse near Eagle City. The tale says that he stashed the loot "forty paces north of the Eagle Creek Bridge, behind a thunder split snag." Unfortunately, since the area tends to flood, the river changes direction and multiple fires have raged the area since Cassidy was there, any "thunder split snag" will have disappeared by now, leaving the coins mysteriously hidden. Maybe an unsuspecting hiker will find his loot someday.

The Cassiday Gang

Some of the hardest criminals the Coeur d'Alene and Spokane officers ever tried to catch belonged to a group of thugs called the Cassiday Gang, and they were on the run in 1908. They made their mark by committing a string of simple streetcar hold-ups. Wilson "Stump" Cassiday was the leader of the group. The other members of his gang were George "Squint" Dively, "Slip" Burch, Virgil Fitzgerald and Clark "Frisco" Yarnell.

It was in a dark saloon in Coeur d'Alene that the group decided to commit another robbery—one that would go terribly wrong for them.

As they stood at the end of the bar, sipping their whiskey, which they paid for with stolen money, they flipped a coin to see which one of them would carry the gun. Then they got in their car and drove out to the Union Park area, where they waited patiently. Their target was a streetcar that did not have too many passengers—although it would have less money, there would be fewer witnesses.

Around midnight, streetcar no. 28 of the Almont Line slowly moved through the park and stopped at the corner of Webster and Laura Streets. It carried only a couple of passengers, so the gang thought this would be the one to rob. Aboard were Conductor George Smith, Motorman John Cong, Dr. W.H Cummings (a dentist in Coeur d'Alene), J.H. Alester and his young son. As the gang approached the streetcar, one of them shoved the gun into the stomach of the frightened conductor. The quick-thinking Cummings grabbed the gun from the men and punched another in the jaw. The one with the gun lost his balance and fell, and as he went down, the gun discharged. The bullet lodged itself in Cumming's right leg, shattering his knee. More bullets were fired, breaking a few windows. The gang took off running toward the north end of the park.

Cumming hobbled as best he could toward a nearby friend's house on Perry Street; the friend was a physician. The passengers, Alester and his young boy, were luckily unharmed.

Cassiday was sponging off a young Chinese girl named Minnie Watson. He sweet-talked her by promising he would marry her if she stayed with him. She was a part-time prostitute, but she was known to steal jewelry as well. All of the money she earned or stole she handed over to Cassiday.

Detectives Miles, Macdonald and Pugh eventually found the whereabouts of the Cassiday Gang and planned their arrests. The gang was staying at the local Rainier-Grand Hotel. One night, when they were enjoying a show at the Coeur d'Alene Theater, the officers arrested the oblivious gang members. For some reason, Yarnell was not present at the show.

When Deputy Don Kizer interviewed Cassiday, he told him he was going to charge him with vagrancy. Cassiday objected sternly and spat, "I'll stand pat on all charges except that of living off the earnings of a prostitute!"

When Burch was interviewed, he quickly ratted out Cassiday with enough information that Cassiday would easily end up in the state penitentiary. Fitzgerald's father was a prominent attorney in Spokane and was not at all pleased with his son's illegal actions.

Judge Huneke of the superior court did not have much patience for the gang.

Cassiday finally pled guilty to living off the earnings of a fallen woman but would not confess to any of the streetcar hold-ups. The judge smacked down his gavel and gave Cassiday a sentence in the state penitentiary from one to five years and a $1,000.00 fine. Burch did not confess to the streetcar robbery either, but he pleaded guilty to a charge of robbing Frank DeFoe for $4.50 in January, when he was walking east on the Sprague Avenue Trestle. Dively fessed up to the Hillyard Streetcar hold-up, in which he managed to steal $10.00 off of S.H. Wardell.

Yarnell was eventually located in Tacoma, Washington, where Sheriff Deputies Lang and Pugh went to get him. Yarnell confessed to robbing the wallet of Conductor Wardell in the Hillyard incident and even offered to show the police where he stashed it. When the officers drove to the corner of Ash and Indiana Streets, the wallet was right where Yarnell said it would be.

The hard work of the never-tiring officers and detectives brought a final end to the reign of terror the Cassiday Gang brought to Coeur d'Alene.

No later records can be found of the prostitute Minnie Watson.

COEUR D'ALENE ROBBER LEAVES MOSTLY EMPTY-HANDED

In late January 1908, a very unlucky robber attempted to violate most of the stores on Fourth Street, as well as a few others nearby. Fortunately for the business owners, yet unfortunately for the robber, they did not acquire much. The destruction they caused far outweighed any goods they stole.

On January 27, someone had their mind set that they were going to go on a crime spree. They moved from one store to the next, breaking windows and doors, in search of anything of value. The thief broke into the Arnold, Olson & Davis Grocery Store, where there was no money on hand, so the frustrated robber stole a few cigars. Their luck didn't improve when they arrived at the City Meat Market; although the owner had to deal with a broken window, nothing was stolen. The third attempt at robbery was at the Coeur d'Alene Drugstore, where they were able to secure five dollars.

When the perpetrator made their way from Fourth Street to Sherman Avenue, they decided to break into the Model & Norquist Store (below the Antler Hotel). There, they broke through the window, determined to rob the place, but as fate would have it, they accidentally broke a stove pipe, which clattered to the floor below and scared the assailant into running off in fear, empty handed.

No arrests were ever made.

GAMBLERS

Gambling was, for many, a means of gainful employment, but for most, it led to destruction, frustration and, sometimes, murder. Some things never change; the odds are against you, and the house typically wins. In the early days of Coeur d'Alene, a lot of the buildings were considered brothels, saloons or dance halls, and pretty much all of them offered liquor, sex and gambling.

During Prohibition, there were daily and nightly raids on establishments that were suspected of serving alcohol, and the fines were usually around $300, and perpetrators often spent three months in jail.

As fun as it was, gambling could often cause trouble. Such is the story about a man named F. Stone who, in 1908, was eating at N.E. Bradleys's saloon in Coeur d'Alene called Brad's Place. After dinner, Stone became

A group of unidentified men crowd a saloon in 1900. Women, at this time, were not even allowed in a bar and could be charged with vagrancy. *Courtesy of Wikimedia Commons, unknown photographer, public domain.*

bored and decided to enter a card game at a nearby table. He joined the game for $1.00 and quickly won $7.50. But what Stone didn't know was that there was a prosecuting attorney playing at the table, who later filed a complaint against Brad's Place and Stone. Stone changed his story and said he was never gambling. It seems a bit silly. Was the attorney just a sore loser?

In 1909, Sheriff Bailey of Coeur d'Alene went on a mission to enforce some laws against gambling. He felt things were getting out of control. He wanted to confiscate slot machines and eliminate women being allowed in saloons to drink. He wanted to do away with "box rustling," a form of dishonest activity perpetrated by saloon owners, in which particular women would con the men into buying expensive drinks, and then the woman would get a percentage of the money. For many years in early Idaho, women were not even allowed inside saloons to purchase or drink alcohol. If caught, they faced being arrested and charged with vagrancy.

Gambling in the Coeur d'Alene Mountains was big-time fun and very profitable for most involved. Saloon keepers, prostitutes, hotels—everyone made a few bucks when it came to gambling. Except maybe the men who were losing their paychecks.

"Dutch" Jake: One of the Best Gambling Men of All Time

Jacob "Dutch Jake" Goetz (1853–1927) was deemed the best poker player in north Idaho. He was one of the friendliest, most considerate and non-selfish men to ever live in the Coeur d'Alene region.

Dutch Jake got his start in the mining and railroad camps in the Coeur d'Alene Mountains, although he eventually settled and built his final home in the nearby city of Spokane (Falls) in Washington. He came to the United States from Germany in 1868 with his father and two brothers when he was just a young boy of fifteen years of age. He soon set out to make his mark in the world.

And that he did. In 1874, he moved to Wyoming, where he met his best friend and business partner for life, Harry Baer (1852–1932). The two men would embark on a grand and profitable life together. The two men traveled around north Idaho and soon discovered a fairly easy way to make money. They would provide food and lodging to the men working on the railroads and in mining camps. In 1883, they discovered Murray (a small town east of Coeur d'Alene), and they found a great need there for comfortable and affordable housing for the workers. Some were sleeping in mere canvas tents in the freezing-cold weather. Dutch Jake never liked to see a working man struggling to survive. (It was told he would front some men money on their stakes just to keep them comfortable.) Dutch Jake and Baer liked the town of Murray very much, so they set up a saloon and hotel there that became very profitable.

One of Dutch Jake and Baer's business mottos was to provide the four "Bs" to their customers: bed, booze, board and betting! They refused to ever include the fifth "B" in their business ventures: brothels. Even without brothels, Dutch Jake earned the title of a tenderloin boss, as his establishments were often the center of all the excitement.

In 1885, the pair was smart enough to invest in the Bunker Hill and Sullivan Mine, which was soon to be ridiculously profitable, and they became wealthy beyond their wildest dreams. The two men could not believe their good luck; yet during their entire lives, they remained kind and considerate to others. They helped almost any man or family in need and became some of the most well-loved and respectable men in the area.

In 1886, Dutch Jake's life would get even better—if that were possible. He decided to marry the love of his life, Louisa Knuth, and the pair began planning one of the grandest weddings ever to be realized in Coeur d'Alene. No expense was spared for the grand gala, and Dutch Jake made sure everyone in Coeur d'Alene was invited, no matter what race, religion or economic status the individual had. He posted flyers announcing their wedding on trees and billboards—anywhere he could publicize their celebration.

When the wedding day finally arrived, many shot off dynamite and drank champagne. They partied and ate all day (and all night) long. They lined the streets of Murray, celebrating together until the sun came up. Dutch Jake himself declared, "No sleep until morning!" The group happily obliged. Almost seven hundred people attended their wedding dinner party. This was followed by a parade and a marching band. When morning came and the bright sun shone its face on the town of Murray, many hungover people shielded their eyes.

The business partners invested in many enterprises over the years that involved liquor, housing and gambling. One of their most popular gambling establishments would amuse up to 1,000 people per night. They built the beautiful Coeur d'Alene Hotel in Spokane that would employ 144 people. After the great fire in 1889, the hotel was rebuilt, and this time, it included a fake steamship that was to be placed on the hotel's roof. Their profits and popularity continued.

In 1903, the State of Washington made gambling a felony, but the two men did not fall apart. Instead, they focused on pool and billiards to keep the men entertained. When Prohibition hit, they weathered that storm, too. Dutch Jake always remained in control and positive. He was respectful to police and understood their raids. He never believed in serving minors or drunken women anyway. It was said Dutch Jake actively avoided two things in his life: lawyers and doctors—both of which he could do without.

One of the interesting personality traits of Dutch Jake was that he was a bit of a pyromaniac. He loved anything that could be lit on fire or be blown up. He loved firing his cannon, even though it landed him in jail a time or two. (One of his cannons can be seen today at the Northwest Museum of Arts and Culture in Spokane.)

Dutch Jake was well known for his wild and extravagant parties and picnics. In 1899, he celebrated his fourth annual picnic, which was classified as one of his best. The party began at 7:00 a.m. sharp, and over two hundred men in costume gathered on the corner of Front Avenue and Howard Street; then they moved down Riverside Street until they reached the Northern Pacific Depot, where they boarded the train to downtown Coeur d'Alene. The event lasted the entire weekend and included a pyrotechnical Spanish battle presentation on the Coeur d'Alene Lake that amused and delighted his guests. The fake battle ended when his flagship

Olympia stormed the point at Tubb's Hill with more cannons and many bright lights and fireworks. Music could be heard from far away and was presented by Our Little German Band. Even a circus was erected at Fort Sherman, followed by another grand feast. At midnight, there was a Sitting Bull Ghost Dance to entertain those who were still awake.

In 1902, another grand picnic was planned for the first week of August. This event outdid some of the others with the inclusion of hot air balloons and parachute jumpers. It was held at Sander's Beach and again lasted all weekend. The Coeur d'Alene "Braves" would enjoy boat rides on the Coeur d'Alene Lake, fireworks, torpedo explosions and another faux battle between Spanish war vessels.

Dutch Jake was one of the wildest, biggest partiers and gamblers in Coeur d'Alene's history, and he loved to make people happy.

SWINDLERS

A gang of swindlers raged the outskirts of Coeur d'Alene in 1909 in a real estate scheme that left Chief McGovern irritated and ready to make an arrest. The gang preyed on farmers and their land. The scheme consisted of the leader of the gang driving out to wealthy farms and expressing the desire to purchase the farm. A deal was then drawn up and a deposit was given to the farmer. It was agreed that the farmer would keep the money, with the promise that the men would return with the balance in a few days. While the leader kept the farmer engrossed in his sudden good fortune, the farmer did not realize that the crooks then had a copy of his signature.

The same swindlers then blazed through downtown Coeur d'Alene, where they forged the victim's name on $200 notes, which they promptly cashed at the Exchange National Bank. Nick LaFranz was one of the victims whose name was forged. The handwritten signature was so well forged that even the tellers at the bank could not tell the difference.

The swindlers continued this fraudulent practice successfully throughout the area for some time. They were never apprehended by McGovern.

Speede Escapes

One of the more popular Coeur d'Alene swindlers of the time was a lowlife named H.J. Speede. A sneaky con man, Speede was mostly known for his forgery and bad checks skills around Coeur d'Alene. He easily passed off a bad $0.15 check to J.F. Goldsmith. He then forged another four checks by signing the name of a well-respected, hardworking local plasterer named John Carr, all of them made out to Speede. Those checks were written for amounts between $13.35 and $30.00 each.

Probably the most memorable thing Speede did was somehow escape from his jail cell.

Once captured, Speede was placed in the old city jail but was later found trying to cut his way out by sawing through the bars. Eager to try out their new jail (which had bars made from a stronger metal), the authorities moved Speede to the new prison, determined to teach him a lesson. While the guard was away for just a minute, Speede somehow managed to break the padlock that was keeping him confined. He left a strange letter addressed to Chief McGovern that read, "Speede got out, how did he do it?"

The angry McGovern quickly rounded up some men to find Speede. As suspected, he was at the depot, waiting to board a train that was heading for Spokane. He reluctantly pleaded guilty to his crime and found his way back in the new jail.

Although Speede wasn't known for much other than being a con artist and forger, he did manage to secure some small fame as the first prisoner to break out of the new city jail.

A Slimy Politician

Most people agree politicians are mostly crooked and greedy, but a man named Avery C. Moore of Coeur d'Alene quickly made it to the top of the local list. Not only was he an untrustworthy politician, but he was also an irresponsible husband. At one time, Moore seemed to have it all, as he purchased land in the desirable and wealthy Lake Shore Addition. He was able to pick out and buy several fine lots that provided great views of the lake on which he planned to build a grand and spectacular home. To many, it seemed Moore was on the top of the world.

But just a year later, it was discovered that during his time in the Coeur d'Alene Mountains, Moore had fabricated his own job and said he was involved in the mining business as a "promoter." He also gambled a lot. He passed off many false and forged checks, one of which was used to swindle George Barker out of $100. He told his wife that he needed to return to

Mexico for business, but he was never to return, leaving her destitute and bewildered. Soon, after months of not hearing from her husband and fearing the worst, she had to resort to selling her home furnishings to survive.

She found out that he was wanted in the nearby towns of Sandpoint and Spokane (and as far away as Tacoma, Washington) on charges of fraud and forgery. Much to her dismay, she packed her remaining belongings and headed back to her parents' home in Montgomery, Alabama, on June 11, 1908.

Moore simply disappeared and was never heard from again. Most locals speculated that he simply moved to Mexico to avoid being arrested in Idaho for his crimes.

THE THREE MASKED BANDITS

Faro was a very popular game in Idaho during the late 1800s and 1900s. It is one of the oldest gambling games, played with a deck of cards. A bet is placed by picking a rank, or number, of a card that is drawn from a box or container. Much like poker, there is only one banker.

On a cold night in 1893, in a gambling hall in Coeur d'Alene, three rugged-looking men charged in around midnight, after closing time, and yelled, "Hand's up, quick!" The unsuspecting patrons complied and froze as the men held two Winchester rifles and a six-shooter in their faces. The crooks quickly grabbed all the money that was sitting on the Faro table and then slowly walked backward toward the door. The leader waved his gun around and pointed it again at each of the men and warned, "The first son of a bitch that follows us will get his hide full of lead!" Then they were gone.

The thieves were $800 richer in just seconds. A posse was formed, but the trio of bandits were never caught or identified.

The same robbers seemed to want to press their luck, as they did almost the exact same thing the next week at the Club Saloon in Coeur d'Alene, located on the same block as the First National Bank. Again, around closing time, just before midnight, another Faro game was wrapping up. The bar's owner, Dickey, had moved over to the fireplace to warm up, and his partner, Billy Decker, came over and stood next to him. Just then, the three masked men charged into the saloon, waving their guns, and yelled, "Hands up! Don't move!" But the Club Saloon had more patrons than the last bar the criminals had held up. In fact, it had over a dozen men and soldiers there who had spent the long night (and their hard-earned money) gambling.

Unidentified men playing Faro together. In 1893, a saloon called the Club was robbed by masked bandits, and the villains were never captured. *Courtesy of the Library of Congress, item no. 2012646440; photographer, S.T. Melander, 1913.*

The leader of the gang was wearing a long, brown coat and held a Colt revolver. The second man was wearing a rust-colored dark coat and had a double-action Smith & Wesson. The third robber was also wearing a long coat and holding a Winchester rifle. As one bandit shoved his gun into Dickey's and Billy's faces, the leader quickly gathered up all the gold, silver and notes from the Faro table, which amounted to about $650. The patrons observed that he was trembling as he did this. Noticing this, Private Sutherland quipped to the bandit, "Better be careful, or you will shoot someone with that!" He ignored the comment and hastily moved over to the craps table, which held another $200.

Just as before, the men slowly backed out the same door they had entered through and hurried away. Dickey quickly grabbed his own gun, ran outside and began shooting at the three men. Someone rang the fire bell, and twenty minutes later, a posse was formed, with Officer Bechtel in charge. The men headed out in hot pursuit of the robbers. Their first obvious stop was at Fatty Carroll's ranch, where they searched for the

Bandits like this unidentified cowboy in 1887 would rob stores, gambling and dance halls, saloons and hotels—no one was safe from them. People were often killed for less than a dollar. *Courtesy of John C.H. Grabill, public domain, Wikimedia Commons.*

men, but they did not find the bandits. They then moved on to Mrs. Kircheval's place, where they believed one of the suspects, a man named Ed Haverly, worked. Sure enough, Haverly was there hiding from the law. Bechtel quickly handcuffed him. The other two suspects, Jack Dillon and Sam Holloway (also known as Happy Jack), were nowhere to be

After robbing several Coeur d'Alene saloons, the three crooks bought horses for their getaway. These unidentified cowboys from 1889 look like the bandits. *Courtesy of the Idaho State Historical Society, 63-221-139; photographer, Jane E. Gay, public domain.*

found. It was suspected they had somehow gotten aboard a train that was heading back toward Coeur d'Alene and then on to Spokane.

The angry bar owner, Dickey, out of his own pocket, offered a $100 reward for their capture.

Luckily, the two crooks who fled from Mrs. Kircheval's farm that night were not free from the law for long. The good officer Bechtel remained hot on their trail, determined to capture them. He heard through the grapevine that two men who fit the basic descriptions of Dillon and Happy Jack had purchased two horses from a rancher in Belmont, Washington. The rancher told Bechtel that they told him they were heading off toward Whitman County, Washington.

The thieves stopped along the way to ask a stranger where Sam Peterson's ranch was located. Bechtel soon found out about this, too. The posse quickly headed on to Peterson's ranch. Once there, the men quietly dismounted and surrounded the house. Bechtel knocked heavily on the front door. The unsuspecting crooks answered the door and were seized immediately. They were placed in the local jail. At 10:30 p.m. that night, luck would have Bechtel's side once again. He glanced out the window and saw a rancher, Sam Peterson, riding his horse through town, heading toward the jail house.

Bechtel's instincts were on guard, so he slowly and quietly followed Peterson to the lock-up cell. Sure enough, Peterson was hiding behind the building, carrying two six-shooters. He obviously had plans to try to break Happy Jack and Dillon out of their confinement.

Wasting no time, Bechtel arrested Peterson. Then all three men made their way back to Rathdrum, Idaho, to await their punishments. The next morning, Bechtel turned the men over to Sheriff Costello to await their sentencing.

Back in Coeur d'Alene, gamblers and saloon owners could rest easy, knowing the robbers were locked up in jail.

5

LABOR DISPUTES, REVENGE AND RIOTS

The Coeur d'Alene Mountains were rich in silver and gold, and with those precious metals came a lot of troubles. Many tragic stories can be found about men committing murder out of greed for gold and silver. The occupations of hardrock mining and lumber milling created hundreds of jobs for men in the Coeur d'Alene Mountains. The owners of the mines and mills were always trying to pinch a penny or two by lowering wages and increasing hours. Labor riots, shoot-outs and explosions were not unheard of. The promise of riches from gold and silver has a way of making men crazy.

One of the earliest discoveries of gold in Idaho occurred in February 1860, when Captain Elias Davidson Pierce and his friend named Seth Ferrel discovered gold in the North Fork of the Clearwater River. This was the start of long-term mining in Idaho, which made many men into millionaires and made other men DB (dead broke). In 1867, another man named Wilson and his group of prospectors stumbled across some color. The excitement brewed, and the word got out, but the area was too remote for even the hardiest of men to travel to.

Then, in 1880, A.J. Pritchard discovered gold on Pritchard Creek, near present-day Murray. With the area being more settled during this discovery, men made the trek from as far away as Montana. The trip was discouraging to them, and they felt that the hardship wasn't worth the gain. They turned back, cursing Pritchard's name. But Pritchard was far from being

The mission is located where the Coeur d'Alene River enters Lake Coeur d'Alene. It was built in 1858, and no nails were used. Coeur d'Alene Mission on Lake Coeur d'Alene, 1855; *artist, Gustavus Sohon. Courtesy of Wikipedia, public domain.*

In November 1889, a prospector named Jack Breen discovered gold in the area near Hayden Lake, Idaho. *Courtesy of the Library of Congress, item no. 93503614; artist, Frederic Remington.*

discouraged, as he had seen and gathered gold nuggets in what he termed the "Widow's Claim." He would have the area to himself until the snow began to melt; then, in February, the prospectors started to drizzle in.

Searching for gold was trickier in the Bitterroot Mountains of the northern part of Idaho because the forest was untamed and extremely thick, and any roads available there were nothing more than muddy trails. During that particular winter, the snow was between twelve and twenty feet deep. But the lure of gold in the Coeur d'Alene Mountains was too hard to resist, and in just three months, over five thousand men poured into the area. That rush in 1884 was called the Coeur d'Alene Stampede.

During the 1880s, Idaho's population was one-fourth Chinese, and most were miners. In the 1890s, Japanese laborers started to appear by the thousands in Idaho to work the mines and the railroads. This caused a lot of grief between the laborers, and many confrontations and disagreements ensued between the parties.

In November 1889, a lucky prospector named Jack Breen discovered gold in the area near Hayden Lake. Unfortunately, he did not have any money to work the claim, so he contacted two men named N.R. Palmeter and Jack Osier, who agreed to fund his findings. Unfortunately for the lenders, Breen ended up getting horribly drunk that night while celebrating his future good fortune and somehow died of smoke inhalation. Was he killed by unknown assailants, or was it just a fluke? No one knows. But what is known is that he took the mystery of the location of the gold to his grave.

In 1921, another unsolved murder was committed. An unknown man was shot in the head, and a sack of bricks was tied around his neck. His bloated body was found in Casco Bay in the Coeur d'Alene River. The only clues the police had to work with was that the man was about fifty years old, wore a gray suit, was well dressed, had a flat nose and was bald.

The job of mining was no picnic. Being underground, hundreds (or thousands) of feet deep, digging for ore is one of the most dangerous jobs in the world. While the mine owners were making millions, they quarreled over fifty cents in pay to the men who were risking their lives every day to make them rich. Countless men gave their lives in the mines, many of them nameless and forgotten forever to history. Some men simply signed their names with an "X," either because they did not want people to know who they were, or they could not even write or speak English. If they died and no one came forward to claim their body, they were buried in a very inexpensive and sometimes unmarked grave.

An unidentified worker deep in a mine. While the mine owners got rich, miners had to fight to keep their $3.50 per day wage. *Courtesy of the Library of Congress, item no. 97509734; photographer, H.C. White Co., 1905.*

The men who were mining in Idaho were exposed to more than just danger from the collapse of a shaft or tunnel; they were also exposed to lead poisoning. In the 1920s, they would treat forty men at a time with the Claque electrolytic methods. The men would sit with their arms and legs in saltwater, and then 110 volts of electricity would run through their bodies. Whether this treatment worked or not is unclear, but it was just one more unimaginable thing these hardworking men had to endure.

The Mission Massacre of 1892

Local unions were formed in Idaho in the 1880s, and mine owners specifically developed their own association to gain control of the workers. They wanted to decrease the pay and increase the hours worked by the men. Of course, the hardworking men were not too happy about this arrangement, especially as they watched the mine owners get fat and rich.

In 1891, the miners' wages were $3.50 per day, so when it was threatened that their wages would decrease, the men decided to strike. It is interesting to note that, in 1891, the very profitable Coeur d'Alene region alone had shipped out $4.9 million dollars' worth of lead, silver and gold.

During the strike, the mine owners did not want to stop their operations, so they had trains bringing in "scabs" (men who were willing to cross a picket line) to work. These scabs were often confronted by very angry and armed miners. These fights, many times, resulted in deaths.

One of the worst mining labor disputes in north Idaho's history began in the Silver Valley. When the scabs refused to leave, the disgruntled miners decided to blow stuff up as a warning. A bag of gunpowder caused a huge explosion and completely destroyed the Frisco Mine, injuring several men and causing the death of another. They meant business. When the miners discovered Pinkerton Agent Charles Siringo was a spy, they stormed his house, but luckily, he had escaped through a trapdoor in his floor and run for the safety of the woods. The angry miners demanded the scabs leave, or they would continue to blow things up. They gave the manager of the Bunker Hill mine an ultimatum: the scabs go, or they would blow up the mine.

Soon, 130 scabs were put on trains and sent on their way to safety in Coeur d'Alene. The train stopped at the mission, where the next form of transportation to Coeur d'Alene was a boat. But, as unfortunate circumstances would have it, the steamship *Georgia Oakes* was late, due to the fact that it had been rescheduled earlier in order to take U.S. troops from Fort Sherman to Harrison.

The legend says that while the men waited for the steamship to take them to the safety of Coeur d'Alene, a group of armed men rode up on horses and began shooting at them. The unarmed men panicked and began scattering, fearing for their lives. Many men were shot and were later found in the river, their bodies gutted in a sloppy attempt to sink them. Some of the bodies of the dead were robbed first. Some people believe that no men were killed during this incident, but many reports of these crimes were written in the local papers. (Later, even undercover agent Charles Siringo, 1855–1928, testified that a man named Abbott actually saw the union men robbing the scabs then

Above: Unidentified men mine over one thousand feet underground in extremely unsafe conditions in 1898. They worked ten-hour shifts for a couple of dollars a day. *Postcard courtesy of Mart Albert Howard Papers and Photographs; photograph taken in Colorado.*

Opposite: When the *Georgia Oakes* arrived, only 15 of the 130 men were waiting to sail to Coeur d'Alene; others began hiking the thirty miles toward town. *Courtesy of Wikipedia, public domain.*

crudely cutting the bodies open, exposing their cavities, so that when they threw them in the river, they would hopefully sink to the bottom.)

At 1:30 p.m., when the *Georgia Oakes* finally arrived, only 15 of the 130 frightened men remained standing there, waiting to be barged to Coeur d'Alene. Most of the men, understandably scared to death, decided not to wait and immediately began hiking the thirty long miles toward the city.

On July 13, 1892, Governor Willey declared martial law, hoping to regain some sense of order. The next day, troops from Fort Sherman on Lake Coeur d'Alene came to the rescue, but by then, the miners had left, heading to either Spokane, Washington, or Montana in the other direction. The men who did stay around were promptly arrested.

Tension remained for months, until November, when the mines finally opened back up, and the men resumed working. A prominent businessman, mine owner and secretary of the Mine Owners Association was quoted as saying, "I verily believe that the majority of the men that belong to the unions of the Coeur d'Alenes are good men. Many are of more than ordinary education and intelligence and as good of men as you can find!"

This event would come to be called the Mission Massacre. There were nine nonunion men wounded, and three union men were known to be wounded; the casualty records listed everything from fractured skulls to multiple gunshot wounds.

Undercover Pinkerton agent Charles Siringo testified that union members were robbing the bodies of the scabs, gutting them and then tossing their bodies into the river. *Courtesy of Wikipedia, public domain.*

Some historians claim that no men ever died during this event, but that seems highly unlikely.

Interesting facts:

- Oddly, the bodies of three dead union men and two nonunion men were aboard the train when it moved up to the mine.
- Charles Angelo Siringo (1855–1928) posed as a shoveler named C. Leon Allison during the mining disputes. He later returned to identify some of the troublemakers.

1894 and Forty Masked Men

"Gem," in the mountains, was another small town in the Coeur d'Alene area that was plagued by labor riots. Violence was popular in Gem due to labor disputes between the miners and the mine owners. In the 1890s, frustration between the union, nonunion miners and mine owners was at its limit. Guards holding Winchester rifles, miners threatening to blow up buildings and constant disputes were everyday occurrences during these troubled times.

A local watering hole, Daxon's Saloon, had dozens of bullet holes in its walls to validate the obscene violence. How the bartender didn't get shot when bullets went flying is still a mystery. One unarmed and unfortunate man, John Ward, was shot in his arm while standing near the White & Bender building. A nonunion man named Ivery Bean was also not lucky; as he was standing between the railroad tracks and Jerry Savage's boardinghouse, he was shot and killed. No one ever discovered who the actual killer of Bean was because so many men were shooting in all directions.

After the dust from that particular dispute settled and the miners surrendered, a total of six men were killed, and sixteen were wounded. They were all taken to the nearby town of Wallace for hospital treatment or funeral arrangements. The dead men listed were Ivery Bean, John Starlick, James Hennessey, Harry Cummings, August Carlson and A.T. McDonald.

John Kneebone, an important witness for the state against the union labor rioters during the trial in 1892, was now working as a local blacksmith. Angry miners were constantly bullying and threatening Kneebone, as they felt he was a traitor. Kneebone should have left town, but he stayed, worked and tried to keep to himself. In the summer of

1894, Kneebone would shoe his last horse. The miners never let go of their anger and feelings of betrayal toward him and were out for blood.

On July 3, a group of forty masked and armed men surrounded Kneebone at his blacksmith shop. One of the masked men said, "Well, we've got one of them," and asked for the whereabouts of several other man. Soon, the workers also had Doc Rogers, R.K. Neill, Foreman Crummer, Frank Higgins and Charles West. Somehow, these terrified men were able to escape and flee from their attackers. No one was ever arrested. Kneebone was just thirty-two years old. His body was buried in Wallace, Idaho, on July 6.

In 1894, the Bunker Hill & Sullivan Mine was shut down, as the managers and owners refused to pay the men $3.50 for each ten-hour day. The mine reopened in 1895 as a nonunion facility, which paid its men only $3.00 per day.

1899 Brings More Strikes, Threats and Dynamite

The year 1899 brought with it more mining disputes and labor troubles in northern Idaho. The second horrid labor confrontation was brewing again between the union miners and the mine owners. One of the frustrations from the miners was the fact that the companies took one dollar per month from each man's paycheck to offset the cost of healthcare. Old-school mining was one of the most dangerous jobs that existed, and the men felt they deserved to be taken care of.

Try to imagine being hundreds if not thousands of feet underground, with only a small candle lamp for light; the air quality was extremely bad and the noise close to deafening. The actual process back then simply included two men working as a team—one holding a steel rod, and the other pounding at it every few seconds with an eight-pound hammer. If the worker missed the rod, the person holding that rod would no longer have a hand. Many miners had missing fingers.

The skilled men would pound these holes in the earth and then fill them with sticks of dynamite. Once all the dynamite was in place, the men would evacuate and then explode the charges. Then the men would proceed back into the site and pick through the pieces of rock that had fallen, looking for color. These chunks of rock would then be carted off and taken out of the mine. The entire process was very slow, extremely difficult, horribly dangerous and almost unimaginable to the people working aboveground.

But the mining process during the 1890s began to develop and change dramatically—for the better. The holes were then being drilled with the assistance of an air compressor, making the job one hundred times easier, although the amount of men (muckers) needed to remove the fallen rock increased. The noise did not get any softer, though, and even with earplugs, many miners ended up almost deaf.

The mine owners decided to join their ranks and form a group they called the Mine Owners Association. The miners formed their own group called the Western Federation of Miners. These two groups rarely saw eye to eye.

This dispute was, again, about the lower hourly wage for workers, the discovery of Pinkerton spies placed among the workers and the fact that the union men wanted to force the nonunion men to join their forces. The owners, again, wanted the nearby miners to also work for fifty cents to one dollar less and accept working for more hours; this did not sit well with the men. The bullheaded manager of the mine refused to cater to any union

After the April 29 fiasco, the State of Idaho and the United States Army decided to punish the rioters and determined that "no union men could work in the Coeur d'Alene region" until further notice. *Courtesy of the University of Washington, public domain, Wikimedia Commons.*

The Idaho National Guard was called when things got out of hand. This image shows Idaho National Guard Batteries C and D, 148th Field Artillery. *Courtesy of Geonames, public domain; photographer, Parish.*

men and reported that he would rather shut down again than crumble to their ridiculous demands.

Trouble was soon brewing, and two hundred union miners loaded themselves into three trains and headed west. Along the way, they picked up hundreds of more angry miners, and most were armed. They also carried onto the train several barrels of black gunpowder. Soon, another one hundred men climbed aboard the train; these men brought sticks of dynamite with them—a whopping four hundred pounds' worth of dynamite.

By the time the mob reached Wardner, the group was four hundred men strong. Their destination was the Bunker Hill and Sullivan Mine.

The *Idaho State Tribune* reported in May 1899, "Miners armed with Winchester rifles were dispatched to the mountainside beyond the mill and the work of placing under the mill 3,000 pounds of dynamite (taken from the Frisco Mine at Gem) was commenced."

At 2:30 p.m., the dynamite was strategically and carefully placed, and the fuses were attached. The men who were working there had a warning to get out or die, and they quickly ran out in all directions. Someone began shooting at the men, and James Cheyne and John Smith were subsequently killed. One man, Harry Orchard (who would later go down in history for a high-profile murder case), eagerly lit one of the fuses. Soon, the mill was blown to smithereens, costing the Bunker Hill Mine owners over $250,000. (In hindsight, it would have been cheaper to just pay the men fifty cents more per day.)

Fifteen seconds later, a second huge explosion was felt. The third blast came fifteen seconds after the last one. Some told officials that the noise from the explosions could be heard all the way to Coeur d'Alene.

The two mines were closed, and six hundred men were then without jobs.

Governor Frank Steunenberg declared martial law on May 3, and soon, arrests were being made for the deadly and destructive fiasco. Bartlett Sinclair was appointed to represent Steunenberg in this matter, as the governor was homesick. Sinclair announced, "The entire community, or the male portion of it, ought to be arrested!" So, the arrests began.

The strange part is that, on May 4, Sinclair ordered the soldiers to arrest all men—waiters, bartenders, cooks, preachers, even a doctor and postmaster were arrested. Some of these men had nothing to do with the explosion of the mine. Yet, the men were rounded up and placed in what was called the bullpen in Kellogg. It was a crude and filthy form of a quickly made concentration camp that was formerly an old cattle barn. It even had barbed wire. The conditions were horrible, and three men died (four if you count the one who escaped but later drowned).

From Coeur d'Alene, Tony Tubbs was hired to supply food and beverages for the men. Tubbs was a generous man, good natured and well liked in Coeur d'Alene. His real name was Wilhelm Martin Anthony August Von Tubbe. He was a German immigrant who had come to the United States at the young age of seventeen in the 1880s. In 1883, he quickly claimed eleven lots in town, which sold immediately, but then, he changed his mind and bought the lots back for $200 each. In 1885, the population of the town was 150, and it was considered a "tent town." But Tubbs could see the value of the beautiful land in Coeur d'Alene. He later became the first justice of peace for Coeur d'Alene and opened the town's first hotel, Hotel d'Landing.

The bullpen in Wardner, Idaho, 1889. *Courtesy of T.A. Rickard, from the* Bunker Hill Enterprise *(San Francisco: Mining & Scientific Press), 1921, public domain.*

Tubbs was a good man who always wanted to help, so he was a natural choice when it came time to help the men in need who were imprisoned at the bullpen.

But Barlett Sinclair was still not happy. He hastily hired on-the-spot "deputies" (really just Bunker Hill Mine employees) to find and arrest the men responsible for the explosions. The makeshift deputy hirings became so ridiculous that even a man named Murphy (who was a horse thief and cattle rustler) became one of these so-called deputies. Some of the bullpen convictions were short-lived, and within a few weeks, some of the men were released without any convictions. Others were housed there for months against their will. An interesting note is that the mine owners outwardly begged Steunenberg to help them with the prosecutions. It must have worked because Steunenberg, being a modest and somewhat "poor" man financially, had magically managed to put a whopping $35,000 into his bank account. Was this a bribe?

The Famous Pinkerton Detectives

With the motto "We Never Sleep" (its eye logo started the well-known term *private eye*), it is no wonder that the unstoppable Pinkerton agents became so famous. They were called in to service many problems—everything from bank and train robberies to labor disputes.

The founder, Allan Pinkerton (1819–1884), stumbled on becoming a detective by accident. Later, his company was so successful that President Abraham Lincoln (1819–1884) even hired Allan Pinkerton as his personal bodyguard.

Pinkerton had an interesting history. He was the son of a police sergeant, so crime detection ran in his blood. He started his detective agency in 1850, his cases mostly focusing on railway theft. As fate would have it, he accidentally became a detective when he discovered evidence of counterfeiters while scrounging for wood scraps. He wormed his way into the graces of the criminals to learn more about their movements, and then he turned them into the local sheriff. The counterfeiters were promptly arrested. In 1849, Pinkerton became the first police detective in Chicago.

Pinkerton formed his own agency, and they focused on bank and train robberies and jewel thieves. Their informers were given code names. Working undercover required great detective skills, and the men would

The Pinkerton slogan helped create the term *private eye* for detectives. The Pinkertons consisted of thousands of detectives—and even the first female agent. *Courtesy of* Encyclopedia Britannica.

have to be very secretive under stressful conditions. To be a Pinkerton agent, they would have to possess skills such as being able to blend in and be inconspicuous, gain the trust of laborers and men who were naturally highly suspicious, act and talk like a miner or laborer (not a detective) and, of course, drink with the boys while keeping a tight lip. Being able to maintain their secret identity was the most important aspect of their job, and it could literally mean the difference between life and death. Men did not take kindly to labor spies—and "accidents" could happen, resulting in death. The undercover agents were required to write secret professional reports about the goings-on, working conditions and activities of the workers for the management. They were also employed as henchmen and provocateurs for various government entities and corporations.

The operatives were often given code names such as B65 or Number 37 so that if they were written correspondence that was confiscated or read by outsiders, their identity was protected. Local sympathetic postal workers who supported the union members would often read private letters and telegrams in order to get the dirt on what was going on and share this information with the appropriate authorities.

The famous Pinkerton agent Charles Siringo was called "C. Leon Allison" while working as an operative in the Idaho mines. Siringo was notorious for carrying a silver-plated Colt .44 pistol and a twenty-inch-long throwing knife concealed in his walking stick.

Many Pinkerton agents were involved in the Coeur d'Alene mining disputes and riots.

Only five men ran the Pinkerton Agency from 1850 to 1967. The founder, Allan Pinkerton, had two sons who became involved with the business:

Left: Illustration of Allan Pinkerton from *Harper's Weekly*, July 1884. He formed his own detective agency that employed the first female detective. *Courtesy of the Library of Congress, item no. 96524967.*

Below: Abraham Lincoln, Allan Pinkerton and General James McClernand at the Battlefield of Antietam in Sharpsville, Maryland, in 1862, where twenty-three thousand were killed in a day. *Courtesy of Alexander Gardner, the Library of Congress, item no. scsm000671.*

Unidentified Pinkerton agents gathered after a riot in 1892. The Pinkertons were part of a very famous detective agency that enlisted thousands of brave men. *Drawing courtesy of W.P. Snyder, based on a photograph by Dabbs, Pittsburg.*

William (1846–1923) and Robert (1848–1907). William ran the Chicago branch, and Robert operated the New York branch. Robert's son, also named Allan (1876–1930), managed the New York office after his father died unexpectedly in 1907. Their uncle, also named William, later ran the Chicago office. Allan's son, Robert (1904–1967), was the last of the Pinkertons to ever direct the agency. At the time of Robert's death in 1907, the agency employed over two thousand men (and a few women) and was in charge of protecting over four thousand banks in the United States.

Interesting facts:

- The well-known Pinkerton agents were hired to find, capture and arrest such notorious outlaws as Jesse James (1847–1882), Butch Cassidy (whose real name was Robert LeRoy Parker, 1866–1908) and the Sundance Kid.
- At the time of Allan Pinkerton's death, he was working on the first centralized criminal database ever established, and it is still being used today by the FBI (Federal Bureau of Investigation).
- Allan Pinkerton hired the first female detective. A twenty-three-year-old girl named Kate Warne (1833–1868), who, for

Pinkerton men Pat Connell, William Pinkerton and Sam Finley pose with their rifles for the camera in 1880. *Courtesy of the Library of Congress, item no. ppmsca.10781.*

Above: Allan Pinkerton had two sons, William and Robert Pinkerton. After his death, William ran the Chicago branch, and Robert ran the New York agency. *Courtesy of the* Albuquerque Evening Citizen, *May 11, 1907.*

Right: The well-known Pinkerton agents were hired to find, capture and arrest such notorious outlaws as Jesse James, seen here. *Courtesy of the Library of Congress, item no. 2004672083.*

one stint, played the role of a fortune teller. She was the main person in charge of uncovering the 1861 Baltimore plot to kill President Abraham Lincoln.

- In 1884, when Pinkerton died, his two sons took over the agency. The company had two thousand agents on payroll and over thirty thousand more in reserves—more men in total than the U.S. Army.
- Pinkerton agents were hired to guard and protect Marilyn Monroe's (1926–1962) casket at her funeral.
- The Pinkerton agents are still going strong, even today, as a private security firm.

The Wicked Plot to Blow Up Idaho's Ex-Governor Frank Steunenberg

The horrible death of Idaho's ex-governor Frank Steunenberg (1861–1905), caused by Harry Orchard (1866–1954), left a deep scar on Idaho's history.

Orchard, whose real name was Albert Horsley, was a conniving and ruthless criminal. He had no problem using dynamite to get his point across. He could remain completely unemotional and detached as he caused extreme destruction around him, with no concern of the possibility of killing an innocent victim or two.

Under Orchard's belt was a long list of other crimes he committed…

- He calmly lit one of the fuses that blew up the Bunker Hill & Sullivan mine.
- Built a bomb to destroy the Vindicator Mine at Cripple Creek that killed two men named McCormick and Beck.
- Fired buckshot into the body of Detective Lyle Gregory in Denver, killing him.
- Stalked Governor Peabody and Judge Gebbert in Denver waiting for the opportunity to kill them both
- Planned the blowing up of the railway station at the Independence Mine at Independence, Colorado that killed fourteen men.
- Attempted to kill Fred Bradley (an executive in the Bunker Hill & Sullivan Mine) while he was living in San Francisco, by putting strychnine into his milk when it was left at his door. This plot failed, so in November 1904, he arranged a bomb

Former Idaho governor Frank Steunenberg was killed by a bomb that was planted on the gate to his home. Steunenberg's last words were: "They finally got me." *Courtesy of the* San Francisco Call, *February 20, 1906.*

that blew Bradley into the street when he opened his door in the morning.

- Murdered Arthur Collins in Telluride.

When Orchard was convicted, he told the detectives his life story—some truth and some fiction. He told them that after traveling all around the United States, he settled in at Wallace, Idaho. He watched the tension get worse every day between the union miners and the management in the Coeur d'Alene Mountains. Orchard saw the tension as a way to make a profit. He would travel and participate in violent protests and was eager to make bombs if they were needed (as he did for the Vindicator Mine in Colorado).

Harry Orchard had a long list of crimes under his belt, but later in life, he found God and repented for his sins. He voluntarily remained in prison until his death in 1954. *Courtesy of Wikimedia, public domain.*

Orchard and his friends just could not stay clear of trouble. In Denver, they approached a man who was working for a local mine company that had been known to harass and assault men in the United Mine Workers of America. It was reported that Orchard and his friend Bill Haywood went back to their lodge and grabbed a sawed-off shotgun. They followed the man, and when he stopped in an alley, Haywood filled him with lead.

In 1905, the vicious gang of Charles Moyer, Bill Haywood, George Pettibone and Harry Orchard gathered to plot to kill the ex-governor Steunenberg. Haywood even gave Orchard $300 for travel expenses. Orchard made his way from Denver, to Portland, to Seattle and finally to Caldwell, Idaho, where he began his search for Steunenberg's home. Once he located the home, Orchard devised a horrific plan to blow up Steunenberg at his residence in Caldwell, Idaho. (He later confessed his dreadful plan to Pinkerton Agents James McParland and George Hueber.)

Bill Haywood, Charles Moyer and George Pettibone in 1907, sitting outside the sherriff's office in Boise, Idaho, awaiting trial for the murder of ex-governor Frank Steunenberg. *Courtesy of the Library of Congress, item no. 2004677537.*

The story of the assassination is sketchy, and truthfully, how much the other three men were involved in the murder is unknown. Newspaper stories vary. Who really was the mastermind behind the plot—Orchard, the other men, all of them?

Orchard stalked Steunenberg and wrote down his daily movements and schedules. Steunenberg frequented Boise on business and stayed at the Idanha Hotel. Orchard wanted to place a bomb under his bed at the Idanha Hotel and blow him up, but he quickly abandoned the idea and developed another that he liked better.

Orchard decided he would go to Steunenberg's home on Christmas Eve and shoot him through the window, but again, he changed his mind.

He settled on his final idea: he would build a bomb and place it on the outside gate at the Steunenberg residence, and when the gate was opened, the bomb would explode, killing Steunenberg instantly. So, on the snowy, blistery day of December 30, 1905, the unsuspecting ex-governor went for a walk. Upon his return, he approached the wooden gate attached to his side door. As he pulled the slide and swung the gate open—the bomb exploded. As he lay on the ground in a bloody pulp, Steunenberg's last words were,

The Idanha Hotel in Boise, where murdered governor Frank Steunenberg stayed. Harry Orchard planned on putting a bomb in Steunenberg's room but chickened out. *Courtesy of the Library of Congress, item no. id0006.*

"They finally got me." He meant the Western Federation of Miners finally "got him." Steunenberg was soon dead.

Orchard went on with his life as usual, playing cards and drinking. The police eventually became suspicious of him for the murder of Steunenberg. He tried to clear his name, but to no avail; he was finally arrested for the murder charge. He eventually confessed to the bombing. He also ratted out Charles Moyer, Bill Haywood and George Pettibone (and he ratted out Jack Simpkins, a Western Federation of Miners committee member) for their involvement in the plot, saying they paid him to kill Steunenberg.

Charles Darrow was hired to defend Hayward, Moyer and Pettibone, and since the prosecutor was unable to present any information against the men, they were acquitted by the jury. Orchard did not get so lucky. During the three-month-long trial, it was discovered that Orchard had a second motive for killing Steunenberg. He ultimately blamed Steunenberg for screwing up his plans to make a bunch of money in the mining industry.

Simpkins was nowhere to be found, and the Pinkerton Agency offered a $2,000 reward for him; anyone with information was to call the Spokane agency at the phone number 234.

During his trial, Orchard endured thirty-two and a half hours of examinations. He finally left the stand at 2:30 p.m., after he had identified the casing of the bomb he had built and used at Judge Goddard's home in Denver, Colorado.

In June 1907, Orchard confessed to his sins during a cross-examination conducted by Detective McParland. He noted that tough-guy Orchard began rocking and crying. Orchard said he wanted to come clean and make all possible reparations by offering his confession.

The *Coeur d'Alene Press* printed his confession:

> *I thought of putting myself out of the way (suicide), but I thought over my past life. I did not believe in the hereafter at all, but I was afraid to die and thought of all the times that I have been such a monster. Many of my crimes had been so great that I would not be forgiven. I had been sent a Bible and read it and came to the conclusion that I would be forgiven if I made a confession of everything, and I made up my mind to tell the truth.*

Orchard was sentenced to serve forty-six years at the Idaho State Penitentiary in 1908, although he was originally sentenced to hang. Harry Orchard, because he had provided evidence against the other men, received a sentence of life in prison rather than the death penalty.

When he was offered parole years later, Orchard declined the offer. He said he would rather live out his days within the confines of the prison, which he did until his death in 1954.

CONCLUSION

The early years of Coeur d'Alene were a wild ride, with many salacious events and fascinating people. Even with all the murders and crime back then, the town was still one of the most intoxicating and beautiful places to ever exist.

Today, the beauty of Coeur d'Alene is just as amazing as it was back then. Thousands flock to the city every month to either explore all it has to offer or look for a place to live.

I hope this book has offered you an inside look at the interesting early life of Coeur d'Alene, its nearby towns and all of its colorful characters. I pray that when you visit the city or walk its streets, you will think of these old-timers and their hardships, sacrifices, faith and visions.

If you pass by any of the original Coeur d'Alene buildings from yesteryear, please pause for a moment or two and remember the people who built them and why they did so. If you find yourself at the corner of some of the town's streets, pay your respects to the individuals who lost their lives in those exact spots one hundred years ago.

Coeur d'Alene is a beautiful city with a seedy history, but I ask you: don't all towns have that little bit of wickedness hidden away in their past?

BIBLIOGRAPHY

Articles

Adams, Ken. "Angels or Whores? Prostitutes in the Mining Camps." www.3rd1000.com.

Albuquerque Evening Citizen. "Pinkerton Agency Charged with Persecuting Miners!" May 11, 1907.

Andrews, Evan. "10 Things You May Not Know About the Pinkertons." History. August 22, 2018. www.history.com.

Arksey, Laura. "May Arkwright Hutton Essay." November 16, 2005. www.HistoryLink.org.

Associated Press. "Artifacts May Corroborate Evidence from the 1863 Murder." August 17, 1992.

Cheney, Louise. "Hill Beachy Nightmare and the Murder of Lloyd Magruder." Newspaper article, date unknown.

Coeur d'Alene Eagle. "Stumpy Wicks Is Dead." May 3, 1884.

Coeur d'Alene Evening Press. "Body of Murdered Man Found." December 7, 1909.

———. Franklin Fire information. September 17, 22 and 23, 1908, and October 1, 1908.

———. "Hendershot Crimes." April 20, 1909, and July 1, 1910.

———. "Kyriss Murder Mystery Deepens." July 25,1908; July 26, 1908; and June 1, 1909.

———. "Raid Red Light House." June 16, 1908.

———. "Rathdrum Train Robbery." August 15, 1908.

Coeur d'Alene Press. Bootlegging information. July 8, 1908; May 10, 1910; and June 10, 1910.

———. "Dickey Faro Bank in Coeur d'Alene Robbed." October 21, 1893.

———. "Dickeys Faro Robbery." October 28, 1893.

———. Dutch Jake information. July 22 and 29, 1899, and July 26, 1902.

———. Franklin Fire information. September 22, 1908.

———. "Frank Steunenberg Murder." June 6, 1907.

———. "Jumped the Town." June 18, 1908.

———. "Murphy Goes to Prison." March 18, 1908.

———. O'Leary murder information. October 6, 1894.

———. "The Owl Saloon." April 8, 1905.

———. Speede information. December 26 and 28, 1908.

———. "Suicide or Murder?" August 28 and 29, 1906.

Daily Astorian. O'Leary murder information. June 21, 1893.

Daily Idaho Press. August 26, 1909.

DeArment, R.K. "Two-Gun' Hart: The Prohibition Cowboy." HistoryNet, www.historynet.com.

Encyclopedia Britannica. "Pinkerton National Detective Agency: American Independent Police Force." www.britannica.com.

Evening Bulletin. "The Murderers from Idaho." November 6, 1863.

Filby, Evan. "Magruder Killers Fight Extradition from California." *South Fork Revue*, November 6, 2013, www.sourdoughpub.blogspot.com.

Fisherman & Farmer. O'Leary murder information. June 16, 1893.

GamblingSites. "Faro History and How to Play." www.gamblingsites.com.

Grangeville Globe. "Chinamen Hanged at Pierce." September 11, 1913.

Hansen, Matthew. "Two Gun and Trey and Me." Between Coasts: Stories from the Flyover, August 2019. www.betweencoasts.org.

HistoryLink. Dutch Jake information. www.historylink.org.

Idaho Tri-Weekly Statesman. "Death of Hill Beachy." May 27, 1875.

Ketchum Keystone. "Bold Robbery in Coeur d'Alene." October 21, 1893.

Roizen, Ron. "This Bloody Deed: The Magruder Incident." Hill Beachy Project, 2013. www.roizen.com.

Salt Lake City Tribune. "The Gruber Case." July 7, 1911.

San Francisco Call. "Frank Steunenberg Murder." February 20, 1906.

Smalley, Eugene V. "The Coeur d'Alene Stampede." *Century Magazine*, October 1884.

Spokane Falls Review. "In Jealous Rage." March 7, 1889.

University of Idaho Library. "Molly Eulogy: Molly B'Damn (Maggie Hall)." Idaho's Women of Influence, Digital Initiatives. www.lib.uidaho.edu.

Wikipedia. "Alcohol and Native Americans, Legislation Controlling Access to Alcohol." www.en.wikipedia.org.

———. "Pinkerton Agency." www.wikipedia.org.

Books

Brainard, Wendell. *Golden History Tales from Idaho's Coeur d'Alene Mining District.* Aurora, CO: Kingsbury Foundation, 1990.

Dahlgren, Dorothy, and Simone Kincaid. *In All the West—No Place Like This.* Coeur d'Alene: Museum of North Idaho, 1996.

Dolph, Jerry, and Arthur Randall. *Wyatt Earp and Coeur d'Alene Gold!* Coeur d'Alene: Museum of North Idaho, 2008.

Dougherty, Michael. *Idaho's Famous Ladies of the Night.* Bozeman, MT: Ultimate Press, 2008.

Hutton, May Arkwright. *The Coeur d'Alenes: Or a Tale of the Modern Inquisition in Idaho.* Wallace, ID: self-published, 1900.

Magnuson, Richard G. *Coeur d'Alene Diary*. Portland, OR: Binford & Mort Publishing, 1968.

Moynahan, Jay. *Red Light Revelations: The Sportin' Women of Wallace and the Silver Valley, 1888–1909*. Spokane, WA: Chickadee Publishing, 2001.

North Idaho Memories: The Early Years 1800s–1939. Coeur d'Alene: Coeur d'Alene Press and Museum of North Idaho, 2012.

Seagraves, Anne. *Soiled Doves: Prostitution in the Early West.* Hayden, ID: Wesanne Publications, 1994.

Singletary, Robert. *Teresa Graham: Grand Dame of North Idaho*. Coeur d'Alene, ID: Coeur d'Alene Press, 2020.

Stapilus, Randy. *Outlaw Tales of Idaho*. Guilford, CT: TwoDot Publishing, 2008.

Websites

www.ancestry.com
www.enjoycoeurdalene.com
www.findagrave.com
www.historylink.org

www.HMdb.org (historical marker database)
www.libraryofcongress.org
www.roizen.com
www.wikimedia.org

Miscellaneous

Coeur d'Alene Press. Tabloid: "Coeur d'Alene: 100 Years." 1987.

Encyclopedia Britannica. "Pinkerton National Detective Agency." September 25, 2017.

Hirt, Paul, and Katherine Aiken. "History 422: Lecture 11." Washington State University.

Idaho State Archives. AR 201 Kootenai County. Box: 20155069, Civil–Criminal Case Files, A-COB. 1882–1952. Folder: State of Idaho v. Dr. R.J. Alcorn (AKA A.J. Alcorn).

———. AR 201 Kootenai County. Box: 20155070, Civil–Criminal Case Files, COL-GO. 1882–1952. Folder: State of Idaho v. N.H. Coryell.

———. AR 201 Kootenai County. Box: 20155072, Civil–Criminal Case Files, K-MA. 1880–1952. Folder: State of Idaho v. LaFenirer.

Idaho State Historical Society. "Inmates of the Idaho Penitentiary 1864–1947." Public archives and research, 2008.

Powell, Cynthia S. "Beyond Molly b'Damn: Prostitutes in the Coeur d'Alene's 1880–1911." Master's thesis, Central Washington University, 1994.

Smith, Robert Wayne. "The Coeur d'Alene Mining War of 1892." Office of Publications by Oregon State University Press, 1961.

Wikipedia. "1899 Coeur d'Alene Labor Confrontation." www.wikipedia.com.

Wilkins, Major. "Fort Sherman, Idaho." Reference notebooks of a local historian. Coeur d'Alene Library, 1993.

Wolff, Fritz E. "Industrial Espionage 1890s Style: Undercover Agents in the Coeur d'Alene Mining District." *Mining History Journal* (2002): 42–53.

ABOUT THE AUTHOR

Originally from upstate New York, Deborah Cuyle loves everything about small towns and their history. She has also written *Kidding Around Portland, Oregon*; *Images of Cannon Beach, Oregon*; *Haunted Snohomish*; *Ghosts of Leavenworth and the Cascade Foothills*; *Haunted Everett*; *Ghosts of Coeur d'Alene and the Silver Valley*; *Ghosts and Legends of Spokane*; *Ghostly Tales of Snohomish*; and *The 1910 Wellington Disaster*. Her passions include local history, animals, museums, hiking and horseback riding. She, her husband and her son are currently remodeling a historic house in Wallace, Idaho, and a crumbling circa 1881 mansion in Milbank, South Dakota. Keep an eye out for her next books: *Murder & Mayhem in Spokane* and *Murder & Mayhem in Coeur d'Alene & the Silver Valley*.

Deborah Cuyle lives outside of Coeur d'Alene, Idaho, and loves its fascinating history, waterfront charm, excellent food and friendly people! *Courtesy of the author.*